Culinary Herbs
Their Cultivation, Harvesting, Curing and Uses

M. G. Kains

Culinary Herbs: Their Cultivation, Harvesting, Curing and Uses

Copyright © 2022 Indo-European Publishing

All rights reserved

The present edition is a reproduction of previous publication of this classic work. Minor typographical errors may have been corrected without note; however, for an authentic reading experience the spelling, punctuation, and capitalization have been retained from the original text.

ISBN: 978-1-64439-623-0

CONTENTS

Preface	v
Culinary Herbs	1
A Dinner of Herbs	7
Culinary Herbs Defined	10
History	11
Production of New Varieties	14
Status and Uses	17
Notable Instance of Uses	19
Methods of Curing	20
Drying and Storing	22
Herbs as Garnishes	27
Propagation, Seeds	29
Cuttings	31
Layers	33
Division	34
Transplanting	36
Implements	38
Location of Herb Garden	41
The Soil and Its Preparation	42
Cultivation	44
Double Cropping	45
Herb Relationships	46

The Herb List

Angelica	52
Anise	54
Balm	56
Basil	58
Borage	62
Caraway	64
Catnip	67
Chervil	68

Chives	69
Clary	69
Coriander	70
Cumin	73
Dill	74
Fennel	76
Finocchio	79
Fennel Flower	79
Hoarhound	80
Hyssop	81
Lavender	82
Lovage	83
Marigold	83
Marjoram	85
Mint	88
Parsley	90
Pennyroyal	97
Peppermint	98
Rosemary	99
Rue	100
Sage	102
Samphire	105
Savory, Summer	106
Savory, Winter	107
Southernwood	108
Tansy	108
Tarragon	109
Thyme	111

PREFACE

A small boy who wanted to make a good impression once took his little sweetheart to an ice cream parlor. After he had vainly searched the list of edibles for something within his means, he whispered to the waiter, "Say, Mister, what you got that looks tony an' tastes nice for nineteen cents?"

This is precisely the predicament in which many thousand people are today. Like the boy, they have skinny purses, voracious appetites and mighty yearnings to make the best possible impression within their means. Perhaps having been "invited out," they learn by actual demonstration that the herbs are culinary magicians which convert cheap cuts and "scraps" into toothsome dainties. They are thus aroused to the fact that by using herbs they can afford to play host and hostess to a larger number of hungry and envious friends than ever before.

Maybe it is mainly due to these yearnings and to the memories of mother's and grandmother's famous dishes that so many inquiries concerning the propagation, cultivation, curing and uses of culinary herbs are asked of authorities on gardening and cookery; and maybe it is because no one has really loved the herbs enough to publish a book on the subject. That herbs are easy to grow I can abundantly attest, for I have grown them all. I can also bear ample witness to the fact that they reduce the cost of high living, if by that phrase is meant pleasing the palate without offending the purse.

For instance, a few days ago a friend paid twenty cents for soup beef, and five cents for "soup greens." The addition of salt, pepper and other ingredients brought the initial cost up to twenty-nine cents. This made enough soup for ten or twelve liberal servings. The lean meat removed from the soup was minced and mixed with not more than ten cents' worth of diced potatoes, stale bread crumbs, milk, seasoning and herbs before being baked as a supper dish for five people, who by their bland smiles and "scotch plates" attested that the viands both looked "tony" and tasted nice.

I am glad to acknowledge my thanks to Mr. N. R. Graves of Rochester, N. Y., and Prof. R. L. Watts of the Pennsylvania State Agricultural College, for the photographic illustrations, and to Mr. B. F. Williamson, the Orange Judd Co.'s artist, for the pen and ink drawings which add so much to the value, attractiveness and interest of these pages.

If this book shall instill or awaken in its readers the wholesome though "cupboard" love that the culinary herbs deserve both as permanent residents of the garden and as masters of the kitchen, it will have accomplished the object for which it was written.

M. G. Kains

New York, 1912

CULINARY HERBS

In these days of jaded appetites, condiments and canned goods, how fondly we turn from the dreary monotony of the "dainty" menu to the memory of the satisfying dishes of our mothers! What made us, like Oliver Twist, ask for more? Were those flavors real, or was it association and natural, youthful hunger that enticed us? Can we ever forget them; or, what is more practical, can we again realize them? We may find the secret and the answer in mother's garden. Let's peep in.

The garden, as in memory we view it, is not remarkable except for its neatness and perhaps the mixing of flowers, fruits and vegetables as we never see them jumbled on the table. Strawberries and onions, carrots and currants, potatoes and poppies, apples and sweet corn and many other as strange comrades, all grow together in mother's garden in the utmost harmony.

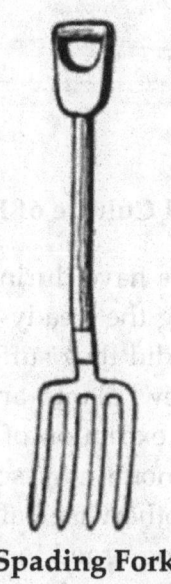

Spading Fork

All these are familiar friends; but what are those plants near the kitchen? They are "mother's sweet herbs." We have never seen them on the table. They never played leading roles such as those of the cabbage and the potato. They are merely members of "the cast" which performed the small but important parts in the production of the pleasing *tout ensemble*—soup, stew, sauce, or salad—the remembrance of which, like that of a well-staged and well-acted drama, lingers in the memory long after the actors are forgotten.

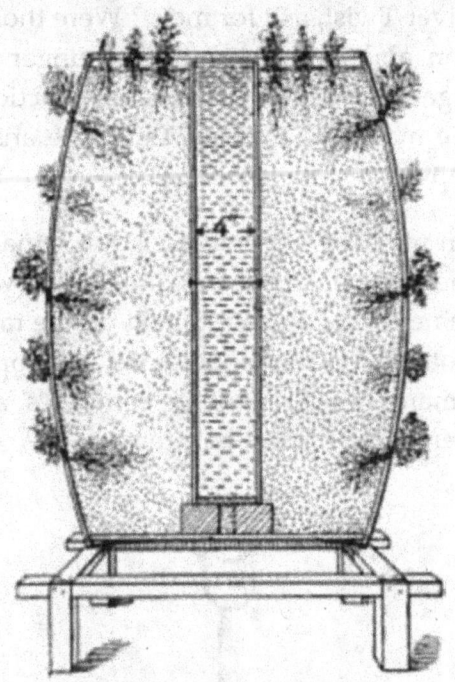

Barrel Culture of Herbs

Probably no culinary plants have during the last 50 years been so neglected. Especially during the "ready-to-serve" food campaign of the closed quarter century did they suffer most. But they are again coming into their own. Few plants are so easily cultivated and prepared for use. With the exception of the onion, none may be so effectively employed and none may so completely transform the "left-over" as to tempt an otherwise balky appetite to indulge in a second serving without being urged to perform the homely duty of "eating it to save it." Indeed, sweet herbs are, or should be the boon of the housewife, since they make for both pleasure and economy. The soup may be made of the most wholesome, nutritious and even costly materials; the fish may be boiled or baked to perfection; the joint or the roast and the salad may be otherwise faultless, but if they lack flavor they will surely fail in their mission, and none of the neighbors will plot to steal the cook, as they otherwise might did she merit the reputation that she otherwise might, by using culinary herbs.

This doleful condition may be prevented and the cook enjoy an enviable esteem by the judicious use of herbs, singly or in combination. It is greatly to be regretted that the uses of these humble plants, which seem to fall lower than the dignity of the title "vegetable," should be so little understood by intelligent American housewives.

In the flavoring of prepared dishes we Americans—people, as the French say, "of one sauce"—might well learn a lesson from the example of the English matron who usually considers her kitchen incomplete without a dozen or more sweet herbs, either powdered, or in decoction, or preserved in both ways. A glance into a French or a German culinary department would probably show more than a score; but a careful search in an American kitchen would rarely reveal as many as half a dozen, and in the great majority probably only parsley and sage would be brought to light. Yet these humble plants possess the power of rendering even unpalatable and insipid dishes piquant and appetizing, and this, too, at a surprisingly low cost. Indeed, most of them may be grown in an out-of-the-way corner of the garden, or if no garden be available, in a box of soil upon a sunny windowsill—a method adopted by many foreigners living in tenement houses in New York and Jersey City. Certainly they may be made to add to the pleasure of living and, as Solomon declares, "better is a dinner of herbs where love is, than a stalled ox with contention."

It is to be regretted that the moving picture show and the soda water fountain have such an influence in breaking up old-fashioned family evenings at home when everyone gathered around the evening lamp to enjoy homemade dainties. In those good old days the young man was expected to become acquainted with the young woman in the home. The girl took pride in serving solid and liquid culinary goodies of her own construction. Her mother, her all-sufficient guide, mapped out the sure, safe, and orthodox highway to a man's heart and saw to it that she learned how to play her cards with skill and precision. Those were the days when a larger proportion "lived happy ever after" than in modern times, when recreation and refreshment are sought more frequently outside than inside the walls of home.

But it is not too late to learn the good old ways over again and enjoy the good old culinary dainties. Whoever relishes the summer cups that cheer but do not inebriate may add considerably to his enjoyment by using some of the sweet herbs. Spearmint adds to lemonade the pleasing pungency it as readily imparts to a less harmful but more notorious beverage. The blue or pink flowers of borage have long been famous for the same purpose, though they are perhaps oftener added to a mixture of honey and water, to grape juice, raspberry vinegar or strawberry acid. All that is needed is an awakened desire to re-establish home comforts and customs, then a little later experimentation will soon fix the herb habit.

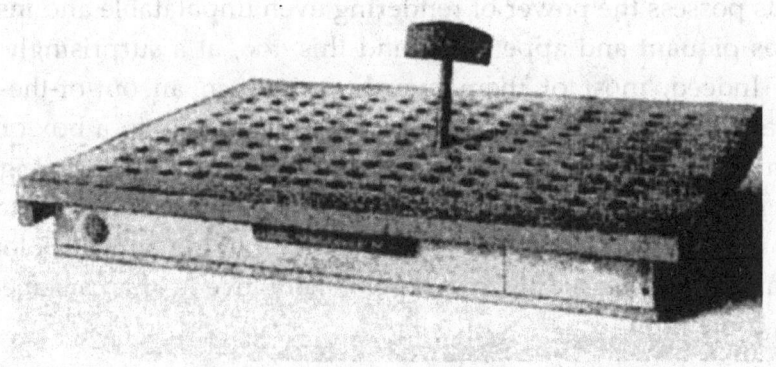

Transplanting Board and Dibble

The list of home confections may be very pleasingly extended by candying the aromatic roots of lovage, and thus raising up a rival to the candied ginger said to be imported from the Orient. If anyone likes coriander and caraway—I confess that I don't—he can sugar the seeds to make those little "comfits," the candies of our childhood which our mothers tried to make us think we liked to crunch either separately or sprinkled on our birthday cakes. Those were before the days when somebody's name was "stamped on every piece" to aid digestion. Can we ever forget the picnic when we had certain kinds of sandwiches? Our mothers minced sweet fennel, the tender leaves of sage, marjoram or several other herbs, mixed them with cream cheese, and spread a layer between two thin slices of bread. Perhaps it was the swimming, or the three-legged racing, or the swinging, or all put together, that put a razor edge on our appetites and made us relish those sandwiches more than was perhaps polite; but will we not, all of us who ate them, stand ready to dispute with all comers that it was the flavors that made us forget "our manners"?

But sweet herbs may be made to serve another pleasing, an æsthetic purpose. Many of them may be used for ornament. A bouquet of the pale pink blossoms of thyme and the delicate flowers of marjoram, the fragrant sprigs of lemon balm mixed with the bright yellow umbels of sweet fennel, the finely divided leaves of rue and the long glassy ones of bergamot, is not only novel in appearance but in odor. In sweetness it excels even sweet peas and roses. Mixed with the brilliant red berries of barberry and multiflora rose, and the dark-green branches of the hardy thyme, which continues fresh and sweet through the year, a handsome and lasting bouquet may be made for a midwinter table decoration, a fragrant reminder of Shakespeare's lines in "A Winter's Tale":

> "Here's flowers for you;
> Hot lavender, mints, savory, marjoram;
> The marigold, that goes to bed wi' the sun
> And with him rises weeping."

The rare aroma of sweet marjoram reminds so many city people of their mother's and their grandmother's country gardens, that countless muslin bags of the dried leaves sent to town ostensibly for stuffing poultry never reach the kitchen at all, but are accorded more honored places in the living room. They are placed in the sunlight of a bay window where Old Sol may coax forth their prisoned odors and perfume the air with memories of childhood summers on the farm.

Other memories cling to the delicate little lavender, not so much because the owner of a well-filled linen closet perfumed her spotless hoard with its fragrant flowers, but because of more tender remembrances. Would any country wedding chest be complete without its little silk bags filled with dried lavender buds and blooms to add the finishing touch of romance to the dainty trousseau of linen and lace? What can recall the bridal year so surely as this same kindly lavender?

A DINNER OF HERBS

In an article published in *American Agriculturist*, Dora M. Morrell says: "There is an inference that a dinner of herbs is rather a poor thing, one not to be chosen as a pleasure. Perhaps it might be if it came daily, but, for once in a while, try this which I am going to tell you.

"To prepare a dinner of herbs in its best estate you should have a bed of seasonings such as our grandmothers had in their gardens, rows of sage, of spicy mint, sweet marjoram, summer savory, fragrant thyme, tarragon, chives and parsley. To these we may add, if we take herbs in the Scriptural sense, nasturtium, and that toothsome esculent, the onion, as well as lettuce. If you wish a dinner of herbs and have not the fresh, the dried will serve, but parsley and mint you can get at most times in the markets, or in country gardens, where they often grow wild.

"Do you know, my sister housewife, that if you were to have a barrel sawed in half, filled with good soil, some holes made in the side and then placed the prepared half barrel in the sun, you could have an herb garden of your own the year through, even if you live in a city flat? In the holes at the sides you can plant parsley, and it will grow to cover the barrel, so that you have a bank of green to look upon. On the top of the half barrel plant your mint, sage, thyme and tarragon. Thyme is so pleasing a plant in appearance and fragrance that you may acceptably give it a place among those you have in your window for ornament.

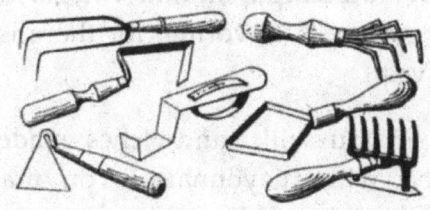

Assortment of Favorite Weeders

"The Belgians make a parsley soup that might begin your dinner, or rather your luncheon. For the soup, thicken flour and butter together as for drawn butter sauce, and when properly cooked thin to soup consistency with milk. Flavor with onion juice, salt and pepper. Just before serving add enough parsley cut in tiny bits to color the soup green. Serve croutons with this.

"For the next course choose an omelette with fine herbs. Any cookbook will give the directions for making the omelette, and all that will be necessary more than the book directs is to have added to it minced thyme, tarragon and chives before folding, or they may be stirred into the omelette before cooking.

"Instead of an omelette you may have eggs stuffed with fine herbs and served in cream sauce. Cut hard-boiled eggs in half the long way and remove the yolks. Mash and season these, adding the herbs, as finely minced as possible. Shape again like yolks and return to the whites. Cover with a hot cream sauce and serve before it cools. Both of these dishes may be garnished with shredded parsley over the top.

"With this serve a dish of potatoes scalloped with onion. Prepare by placing in alternate layers the two vegetables; season well with salt, pepper and butter, and then add milk even with the top layer. This dish is quite hearty and makes a good supper dish of itself.

"Of course you will not have a meal of this kind without salad. For this try a mixture of nasturtium leaves and blossoms, tarragon, chives, mint, thyme and the small leaves of the lettuce, adding any other green leaves of the spicy kind which you find to taste good. Then dress these with a simple oil and vinegar dressing, omitting sugar, mustard or any such flavoring, for there is spice enough in the leaves themselves.

"Pass with these, if you will, sandwiches made with lettuce or nasturtium dressed with mayonnaise. You may make quite a different thing of them by adding minced chives or tarragon, or thyme, to the mayonnaise. The French are very partial to this manner of compounding new sauces from the base of the old one. After you do it a few times you also will find it worth while.

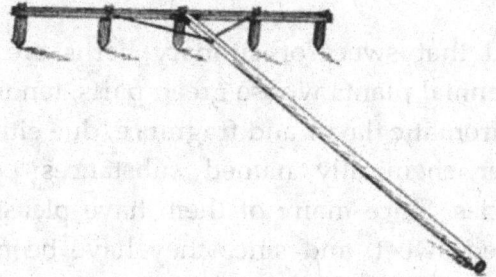

Popular Adjustable Row Marker

"When it comes to a dessert I am afraid you will have to go outside of herbs. You can take a cream cheese and work into it with a silver knife any of these herbs, or any two of them that agree with it well, and serve it with toasted crackers, or you can toast your crackers with common cheese, grating above it sage and thyme."

Whether this "dinner of herbs" appeals to the reader or not, I venture to say that no housewife who has ever stuffed a Thanksgiving turkey, a Christmas goose or ducks or chickens with home-grown, home-prepared herbs, either fresh or dried, will ever after be willing to buy the paper packages or tin cans of semi-inodorous, prehistoric dust which masquerades equally well as "fresh" sage, summer savory, thyme or something else, the only apparent difference being the label.

To learn to value herbs at their true worth one should grow them. Then every visitor to the garden will be reminded of some quotation from the Bible, or Shakespeare or some other repository of interesting thoughts; for since herbs have been loved as long as the race has lived on the earth, literature is full of references to facts and fancies concerning them. Thus the herb garden will become the nucleus around which cluster hoary legends, gems of verse and lilts of song, and where one almost stoops to remove his shoes, for

"The wisdom of the ages Blooms anew among the sages."

CULINARY HERBS DEFINED

It may be said that sweet or culinary herbs are those annual, biennial or perennial plants whose green parts, tender roots or ripe seeds have an aromatic flavor and fragrance, due either to a volatile oil or to other chemically named substances peculiar to the individual species. Since many of them have pleasing odors they have been called sweet, and since they have been long used in cookery to add their characteristic flavors to soups, stews, dressings, sauces and salads, they are popularly called culinary. This last designation is less happy than the former, since many other herbs, such as cabbage, spinach, kale, dandelion and collards, are also culinary herbs. These vegetables are, however, probably more widely known as potherbs or greens.

HISTORY

It seems probable that many of the flavoring herbs now in use were similarly employed before the erection of the pyramids and also that many then popular no longer appear in modern lists of esculents. Of course, this statement is based largely upon imperfect records, perhaps, in many cases only hints more or less doubtful as to the various species. But it seems safe to conclude that a goodly number of the herbs discussed in this volume, especially those said to be natives of the Mediterranean region, overhung and perfumed the cradle of the human race in the Orient and marked the footsteps of our rude progenitors as they strode more and more sturdily toward the horizon of promise. This idea seems to gain support also from the fact that certain Eastern peoples, whom modern civilization declares to have uneducated tastes, still employ many herbs which have dropped by the wayside of progress, or like the caraway and the redoubtable "pusley," an anciently popular potherb, are but known in western lands as troublesome weeds.

Relying upon Biblical records alone, several herbs were highly esteemed prior to our era; in the gospels of Matthew and Luke reference is made to tithes of mint, anise, rue, cummin and other "herbs"; and, more than 700 years previously, Isaiah speaks of the sowing and threshing of cummin which, since the same passage (Isaiah xxviii, 25) also speaks of "fitches" (vetches), wheat, barley and "rie" (rye), seems then to have been a valued crop.

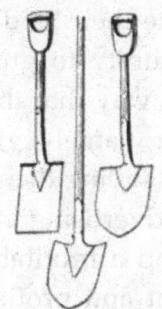

Popular Spades

The development of the herb crops contrasts strongly with that of the other crops to which reference has just been made. Whereas these latter have continued to be staples, and to judge by their behavior during the last century may be considered to have improved in quality and yield since that ancient time, the former have dropped to the most subordinate position of all food plants. They have lost in number of species, and have shown less improvement than perhaps any other groups of plants cultivated for economic purposes. During the century just closed only one species, parsley, may be said to have developed more than an occasional improved variety. And even during this period the list of species seems to have been somewhat curtailed—tansy, hyssop, horehound, rue and several others being considered of too pronounced and even unpleasant flavor to suit cultivated palates.

With the exception of these few species, the loss of which seems not to be serious, this absence of improvement is to be regretted, because with improved quality would come increased consumption and consequent beneficial results in the appetizing flavor of the foods to which herbs are added. But greatly improved varieties of most species can hardly be expected until a just appreciation has been awakened in individual cultivators, who, probably in a majority of cases, will be lovers of plants rather than men who earn their living by market gardening.

Until the public better appreciates the culinary herbs there will be a comparatively small commercial demand; until the demand is sufficient to make growing herbs profitable upon an extensive scale, market gardeners will devote their land to crops which are sure to pay well; hence the opportunity to grow herbs as an adjunct to gardening is the most likely way that they can be made profitable. And yet there is still another; namely, growing them for sale in the various prepared forms and selling them in glass or tin receptacles in the neighborhood or by advertising in the household magazines. There surely is a market, and a profitable one if rightly managed. And with right management and profit is to come desire to have improved varieties. Such varieties can be developed at least as readily as the wonderful modern chrysanthemum has been developed from an insignificant little wild flower not half as interesting or promising originally as our common oxeye daisy, a well-known field weed.

Not the least object of this volume is, therefore, to arouse just appreciation of the opportunities awaiting the herb grower. Besides the very large and increasing number of people who take pleasure in the growing of attractive flowering and foliage plants, fine vegetables and choice fruits, there are many who would find positive delight in the breeding of plants for improvement—the origination of new varieties—and who would devote much of their leisure time to this work—make it a hobby—did they know the simple underlying principles. For their benefit, therefore, the following paragraphs are given.

PRODUCTION OF NEW VARIETIES

Besides the gratification that always accompanies the growing of plants, there is in plant breeding the promise that the progeny will in some way be better than the parent, and there is the certainty that when a stable variety of undoubted merit has been produced it can be sold to an enterprising seedsman for general distribution. In this way the amateur may become a public benefactor, reap the just reward of his labors and keep his memory green!

The production of new varieties of plants is a much simpler process than is commonly supposed. It consists far more in selecting and propagating the best specimens than in any so-called "breeding." With the majority of the herbs this is the most likely direction in which to seek success.

Suppose we have sown a packet of parsley seed and we have five thousand seedlings. Among these a lot will be so weak that we will naturally pass them by when we are choosing plantlets to put in our garden beds. Here is the first and simplest kind of selection. By this means, and by not having space for a great number of plants in the garden, we probably get rid of 80 per cent of the seedlings—almost surely the least desirable ones.

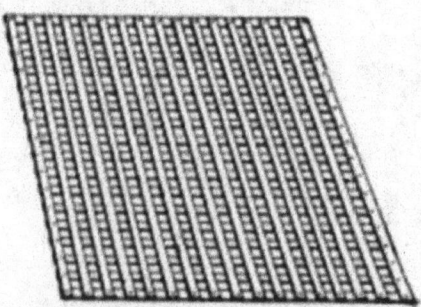

Lath Screen for Shading Beds

Suppose we have transplanted 1,000 seedlings where they are to grow and produce leaves for sale or home use. Among these, provided the seed has been good and true, at least 90 per cent will be about alike in appearance, productivity and otherwise. The remaining plants may show variations so striking as to attract attention. Some may be tall and scraggly, some may be small and puny; others may be light green, still others dark green; and so on. But there may be one or two plants that stand out conspicuously as the best of the whole lot. These are the ones to mark with a stake so they will not be molested when the crop is being gathered and so they will attain their fullest development.

These best plants, and only these, should then be chosen as the seed bearers. No others should be allowed even to produce flowers. When the seed has ripened, that from each plant should be kept separate during the curing process described elsewhere. And when spring comes again, each lot of seed should be sown by itself. When the seedlings are transplanted, they should be kept apart and labeled No. 1, No. 2, No. 3, etc., so the progeny of each parent plant can be known and its history kept.

The process of selecting the seedlings the second year is the same as in the first; the best are given preference, when being transplanted. In the beds all sorts of variations even more pronounced than the first year may be expected. The effort with the seedlings derived from each parent plant should be to find the plants that most closely resemble their own parents, and to manage these just as the parents were managed. No other should be allowed to flower.

This process is to be continued from year to year. If the selection is carefully made, the grower will soon rejoice, because he will observe a larger and a larger number of plants approaching the type of plant he has been selecting for. In time practically the whole plantation will be coming "true to type," and he will have developed a new variety. If his ideal is such as to appeal to the practical man—the man who grows parsley for money—and if the variety is superior to varieties already grown, the originator will have no difficulty in disposing of his stock of seed and plants, if he so desires, to a seedsman, who will gladly pay a round price in order to have exclusive control of the "new creation." Or he may contract with a seedsman to grow seed of the new variety for sale to the trade.

Harvesting Thyme Grown on a Commercial Scale

It may be said, further, that new varieties may be produced by placing the pollen from the flowers of one plant upon the pistils in the flowers of another and then covering the plant with fine gauze to keep insects out. With the herbs, however, this method seems hardly worth while, because the flowers are as a rule very small and the work necessarily finicky, and because there are already so few varieties of most species that the operation may be left to the activities of insects. It is for this reason, however, that none but the choicest plants should be allowed to bloom, so none but desirable pollen may reach and fertilize the flowers of the plants to be used as seed producers.

STATUS AND USES

Some readers of a statistical turn of mind may be disappointed to learn that figures as to the value of the annual crops of individual herbs, the acreage devoted to each, the average cost, yield and profit an acre, etc., are not obtainable and that the only way of determining the approximate standing of the various species is the apparent demand for each in the large markets and stores.

Unquestionably the greatest call is for parsley, which is used in restaurants and hotels more extensively as a garnish than any other herb. In this capacity it ranks about equal with watercress and lettuce, which both find their chief uses as salads. As a flavoring agent it is probably less used than sage, but more than any of the other herbs. It is chiefly employed in dressings with mild meats such as chicken, turkey, venison, veal, with baked fish; and for soups, stews, and sauces, especially those used with boiled meats, fish and fricassees of the meats mentioned. Thus it has a wider application than any other of the culinary herbs.

Sage, which is a strongly flavored plant, is used chiefly with such fat meats as pork, goose, duck, and various kinds of game. Large quantities are mixed with sausage meat and, in some countries, with certain kinds of cheese. Throughout the United States it is probably the most frequently called into requisition of all herbs, probably outranking any two of the others, with the exception of parsley.

Garden Hoes of Various Styles

Thyme and savory stand about equal, and are chiefly used like parsley, though both, especially the former, are used in certain kinds of sausage. Marjoram, which is similarly employed, comes next, then follow balm, fennel, and basil. These milder herbs are often mixed for much the same reason that certain simple perfumes are blended—to produce a new odor—combinations of herbs resulting in a new compound flavor. Such compounds are utilized in the same way that the elementary herbs are.

In classes by themselves are tarragon and spearmint, the former of which is chiefly used as a decoction in the flavoring of fish sauces, and the latter as the universal dressing with spring lamb. Mint has also a more convivial use, but this seems more the province of the W. C. T. U. than of this book to discuss.

Dill is probably the most important of the herbs whose seeds, rather than their leaves, are used in flavoring food other than confectionery. It plays its chief role in the pickle barrel. Immense quantities of cucumber pickles flavored principally with dill are used in the restaurants of the larger cities and also by families, the foreign-born citizens and their descendants being the chief consumers. The demand for these pickles is met by the leading pickle manufacturers who prepare special brands, generally according to German recipes, and sell them to the delicatessen and the grocery stores. If they were to rely upon me for business, they would soon go bankrupt. To my palate the dill pickle appeals as almost the acme of disagreeableness.

NOTABLE INSTANCE OF USES

The flavors of the various herbs cover a wide range, commencing with fennel and ending with sage, and are capable of wide application. In one case which came under my observation, the cook made a celery-flavored stew of some meat scraps. Not being wholly consumed, the surviving debris appeared a day or two later, in company with other odds and ends, as the chief actor in a meat pie flavored with parsley. Alas, a left-over again! "Never mind," mused the cook; and no one who partook of the succeeding stew discovered the lurking parsley and its overpowered progenitor, the celery, under the effectual disguise of summer savory. By an unforeseen circumstance the fragments remaining from this last stew did not continue the cycle and disappear in another pie. Had this been their fate, however, their presence could have been completely obscured by sage. This problem in perpetual progression or culinary homeopathy can be practiced in any kitchen. But hush, tell it not in the dining-room!

Dried Herbs in Paper and Tin

METHODS OF CURING

Culinary herbs may be divided into three groups; those whose foliage furnishes the flavor, those whose seed is used and those few whose roots are prepared. In the kitchen, foliage herbs are employed either green or as decoctions or dried, each way with its special advocates, advantages and applications.

Green herbs, if freshly and properly gathered, are richest in flavoring substances and when added to sauces, fricassees, stews, etc., reveal their freshness by their particles as well as by their decidedly finer flavor. In salads they almost entirely supplant both the dried and the decocted herbs, since their fresh colors are pleasing to the eye and their crispness to the palate; whereas the specks of the dried herbs would be objectionable, and both these and the decoctions impart a somewhat inferior flavor to such dishes. Since herbs cannot, however, always be obtained throughout the year, unless they are grown in window boxes, they are infused or dried. Both infusing and drying are similar processes in themselves, but for best results they are dependent upon the observance of a few simple rules.

Herb Solution Bottle

No matter in what condition or for what purpose they are to be used the flavors of foliage herbs are invariably best in well-developed leaves and shoots still in full vigor of growth. With respect to the plant as a whole, these flavors are most abundant and pleasant just before the flowers appear. And since they are generally due to essential oils, which are quickly dissipated by heat, they are more abundant in the morning than after the sun has reached the zenith. As a general rule, therefore, best results with foliage herbs, especially those to be used for drying and infusing, may be secured when the plants seem ready to flower, the harvest being made as soon as the dew has dried and before the day has become very warm. The leaves of parsley, however, may be gathered as soon as they attain that deep green characteristic of the mature leaf; and since the leaves are produced continuously for many weeks, the mature ones may be removed every week or so, a process which encourages the further production of foliage and postpones the appearance of the flowering stem.

To make good infusions the freshly gathered, clean foliage should be liberally packed in stoppered jars, covered with the choicest vinegar, and the jars kept closed. In a week or two the fluid will be ready for use, but in using it, trials must be made to ascertain its strength and the quantity necessary to use. Usually only the clear liquid is employed; sometimes, however, as with mint, the leaves are very finely minced before being bottled and both liquid and particles employed.

Tarragon, mint and the seed herbs, such as dill, are perhaps more often used in ordinary cookery as infusions than otherwise. An objection to decoctions is that the flavor of vinegar is not always desired in a culinary preparation, and neither is that of alcohol or wine, which are sometimes used in the same way as vinegar.

DRYING AND STORING

When only a small quantity of an herb is to be dried, the old plan of hanging loose bunches from the ceiling of a warm, dry attic or a kitchen will answer. Better, perhaps, is the use of trays covered with clean, stout manilla paper upon which thin layers of the leaves are spread. These are placed either in hot sunlight or in the warm kitchen where warm air circulates freely. They must be turned once a day until all the moisture has been evaporated from the leaves and the softer, more delicate parts have become crisp. Then they may be crunched and crumbled between the hands, the stalks and the hard parts rejected and the powder placed in air-tight glass or earthenware jars or metal cans, and stored in a cool place. If there be the slightest trace of moisture in the powder, it should be still further dried to insure against mold. Prior to any drying process the cut leaves and stems should be thoroughly washed, to get rid of any trace of dirt. Before being dried as noted above, the water should all be allowed to evaporate. Evaporation may be hastened by exposing the herbs to a breeze in a shallow, loose basket, a wire tray or upon a table. While damp there is little danger of their being blown away. As they dry, however, the current of air should be more gentle.

The practice of storing powdered herbs in paper or pasteboard packages is bad, since the delicate oils readily diffuse through the paper and sooner or later the material becomes as valueless for flavoring purposes as ordinary hay or straw. This loss of flavor is particularly noticeable with sage, which is one of the easiest herbs to spoil by bad management. Even when kept in air-tight glass or tin receptacles, as recommended, it generally becomes useless before the end of two years.

Paper Sacks of Dried Herbs for Home Use

When large quantities of herbs are to be cured a fruit evaporator may be employed, the herbs being spread thinly upon wire-bottomed trays so that an ample current of air may pass through them. Care must be taken to keep the temperature inside the machine below 120 degrees. The greatest efficiency can be secured by placing the trays of most recently gathered herbs at the top, the partially dried ones being lowered to positions nearer the source of heat. In this way the fresh, dry, warm air comes in contact first with the herbs most nearly dried, removes the last vestige of moisture from them and after passing through the intervening trays comes to those most recently gathered.

Hand Cultivator and Scarifier

Unless the evaporator be fitted with some mechanism which will permit all the trays to be lowered simultaneously, the work of changing the trays may seem too irksome to be warranted. But where no changes of trays are made, greater care must be given to the bottom trays because they will dry out faster than those at the top. Indeed in such cases, after the apparatus is full, it becomes almost essential to move the trays lower, because if fresh green herbs, particularly those which are somewhat wet, be placed at the bottom of the series, the air will become so charged with moisture from them that the upper layers may for a time actually absorb this moisture and thus take longer to dry. Besides this, they will surely lose some of their flavoring ingredients—the very things which it is desired to save.

No effort should be made to hasten the drying process by increasing the temperature, since this is likely to result as just mentioned. A personal experience may teach the reader a lesson. I once had a large amount of parsley to cure and thought to expedite matters by using the oven of a gas stove. Suffice it to tell that the whole quantity was ruined, not a pinch was saved. In spite of the closest regulation the heat grew too great and the flavor was literally cooked out of the leaves. The delicate oil saturated everything in the house, and for a week or more the whole place smelled as if chicken fricassee was being made upon a wholesale plan.

Except as garnishes, herbs are probably more frequently used in a dry state than in all other ways put together. Perhaps this is because the method of preparing them seems simpler than that of infusion, because large quantities may be kept in small spaces, and because they can be used for every purpose that the fresh plants or the decoctions can be employed. In general, however, they are called into requisition principally in dressings, soups, stews and sauces in which their particles are not considered objectionable. If clear sauces or soups are desired, the dried herbs may still be used to impart the flavor, their particles being removed by straining.

The method of preparing dill, anise, caraway and other herbs whose seed is used, differs from that employed with the foliage herbs mainly in the ripeness of the plants. These must be gathered as soon as they show signs of maturity but before the seeds are ready to drop from them. In all this work especial care must be paid to the details of cleaning. For a pleasing appearance the seed heads must be gathered before they become the least bit weather-beaten. This is as essential as to have the seed ripe. Next, the seed must be perfectly clean, free from chaff, bits of broken stems and other debris. Much depends upon the manner of handling as well as upon harvesting. Care must be taken in threshing to avoid bruising the seeds, particularly the oily ones, by pounding too hard or by tramping upon them. Threshing should never be done in damp weather; always when the air is very dry.

In clear weather after the dew has disappeared the approximately ripe plants or seed heads must be harvested and spread thinly— never packed firmly—upon stout cloth such as ticking, sailcloth, or factory cotton. A warm, open shed where the air circulates freely is an admirable place, since the natural temperature of the air is sufficient in the case of seeds to bring about good results. Usually in less than a week the tops will have become dry enough to be beaten out with a light flail or a rod. In this operation great care must be taken to avoid bruising or otherwise injuring the seed. The beating should therefore be done in a sheet spread upon a lawn or at least upon short grass. The force of the blows will thus be lessened and bruising avoided.

For cleaning herb seeds sieves in all sizes from No. 2 to No. 40 are needed. The sizes represent various finenesses of mesh. All above No. 8 should be of brass wire, because brass is considerably more durable and less likely to rust than iron. The cloths upon which the herbs are spread should be as large as the floor upon which the threshing is to be done except when the floor is without cracks, but it is more convenient to use cloths always, because they facilitate handling and temporary storing. Light cotton duck is perhaps best, but the weave must be close. A convenient size is 10 x 10 feet.

After the stalks have been removed the seed should be allowed to remain for several days longer in a very thin layer—the thinner the better—and turned every day to remove the last vestige of moisture. It will be even better still to have the drying sheet suspended so air may circulate below as well as above the seed. Not less than a week for the smallest seeds and double that time for the larger ones is necessary. To avoid loss or injury it is imperative that the seed be dry before it is put in the storage packages. Of course, if infusions are to be made all this is unnecessary; the seed may be put in the liquor as soon as the broken stems, etc. are removed subsequent to threshing.

HERBS AS GARNISHES

As garnishes several of the culinary herbs are especially valuable. This is particularly true of parsley, which is probably more widely used than any other plant, its only close rivals being watercress and lettuce, which, however, are generally inferior to it in delicacy of tint and form of foliage, the two cardinal virtues of a garnish.

Parsley varieties belong to three principal groups, based upon the form of the foliage: (1) Plain varieties, in which the leaves are nearly as they are in nature; (2) moss-curled varieties in which they are curiously and pleasingly contorted; and (3) fern leaved, in which the foliage is not curled, but much divided into threadlike parts.

The moss-curled varieties are far more popular than the other two groups put together and are the only ones used especially as garnishes with meat dishes in the hotels and restaurants of the large cities. The plain-leaved sorts cannot be compared in any way except in flavor with the varieties of the other groups. But the fern-leaved kinds, which unfortunately have not become commercially well known, surpass even the finest varieties of the moss-curled group, not only in their exquisite and delicate form, but in their remarkably rich, dark-green coloring and blending of light and shade. But the mere fact that these varieties are not known in the cities should not preclude their popularity in suburban and town gardens and in the country, where every householder is monarch of his own soil and can satisfy very many æsthetic and gustatory desires without reference to market dictum, that bane alike of the market gardener and his customer.

Several other herbs—tansy, savory, thyme, marjoram, basil, and balm—make pretty garnishes, but since they are not usually considered so pleasant to nibble at, they are rarely used. The pleasing effect of any garnish may be heightened by adding here and there a few herb flowers such as thyme or savory. Other flowers may be used in the same way; for instance, nasturtium.

There is no reason why herbs so used should not be employed several times over, and afterwards dried or bottled in vinegar if they be free from gravy, oils, fats, etc., and if in sufficient quantity to make such a use worth while. Other pretty garnishes which are easily obtained are corn salad, peppergrass, mustard, fennel, and young leaves of carrot. But surpassing all these in pleasing and novel effects are the curled, pink, red and white-leaved varieties of chicory and nasturtium flowers alone or resting upon parsley or other delicate foliage. So much by way of digression.

PROPAGATION

SEEDS

Flat of Seedlings Ready to Be Transplanted

Most herbs may be readily propagated by means of seeds. Some, however, such as tarragon, which does not produce seed, and several other perennial kinds, are propagated by division, layers, or cuttings. In general, propagation by means of seed is considered most satisfactory. Since the seeds in many instances are small or are slow to germinate, they are usually sown in shallow boxes or seed pans. When the seedlings are large enough to be handled they are transplanted to small pots or somewhat deeper flats or boxes, a couple of inches being allowed between the plants. When conditions are favorable in the garden; that is, when the soil is moist and warm and the season has become settled, the plantlets may be removed to permanent quarters.

If the seed be sown out of doors, it is a good practice to sow a few radish seeds in the same row with the herb seeds, particularly if these latter take a long time to germinate or are very small, as marjoram, savory and thyme. The variety of radish chosen should be a turnip-rooted sort of exceedingly rapid growth, and with few and small leaves. The radishes serve to mark the rows and thus enable cultivation to commence much earlier than if the herbs were sown alone. They should be pulled early—the earlier the better after the herb plantlets appear. Never should the radishes be allowed to crowd the herbs.

By the narration of a little incident, I may illustrate the necessity of sowing these radish seeds thinly. Having explained to some juvenile gardeners that the radish seeds should be dropped so far apart among the other seeds that they would look lonesome in the bottoms of the rows—not more than six seeds to the foot—and having illustrated my meaning by sowing a row myself, I let each one take his turn at sowing. While I watched them all went well. But, alas, for precept and example! To judge by the general result after the plants were up, the seedsman might justifiably have guaranteed the seed to germinate about 500 per cent, because each boy declared that *he* sowed *his* rows thinly. Nevertheless, there was a stand of radishes that would have gladdened the heart of a lawn maker! The rows looked like regiments drawn up in close order and not, as was desired, merely lines of scattered skirmishers. In many places there were more than 100 to the foot! Fortunately the variety was a quick-maturing kind and the crop, for such it became, was harvested before any damage was done the slow-appearing seedlings, whose positions the radishes were intended to indicate.

CUTTINGS

Glass-Covered Propagating Box

No herbs are so easy to propagate by means of cuttings as spearmint, peppermint, and their relatives which have underground stems. Every joint of these stems will produce a new plant if placed in somewhat moist soil. Often, however, this ability is a disadvantage, because the plants are prone to spread and become a nuisance unless watched. Hence such plants should be placed where they will not have their roots cut by tools used close to them. When they seem to be extending, their borders should be trimmed with a sharp spade pushed vertically full depth into the soil and all the earth beyond the clump thus restricted should be shaken out with a garden fork and the cut pieces of mint removed. Further, the forked-over ground should be hoed every week during the remainder of the season, to destroy lurking plantlets.

The other perennial and biennial herbs may be readily propagated by means of stem cuttings or "slips," which are generally as easy to manage as verbenas, geraniums and other "house plants." The cuttings may be made of either fully ripened wood of the preceding or the current season, or they may be of firm, not succulent green stems. After trimming off all but a few of the upper leaves, which should be clipped to reduce transpiration, the cuttings—never more than 4 or 5 inches long—should be plunged nearly full depth in well-shaded, rather light, porous, well-drained loam where they should remain undisturbed until they show evidences of growth. Then they may be transplanted. While in the cutting bed they must never be allowed to become dry. This is especially true of greenwood cuttings made during the summer. These should always have the coolest, shadiest corner in the garden. The cuttings taken in the spring should be set in the garden as soon as rooted; but the summer cuttings, especially if taken late, should generally be left in their beds until the following spring. They may, however, be removed for winter use to window boxes or the greenhouse benches.

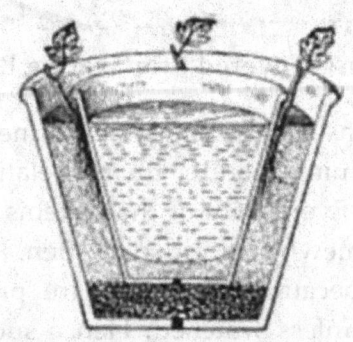

Flower Pot Propagating Bed

Often the plants grown in window boxes may supply the early cuttings, which may be rooted in the house. Where a greenhouse is available, a few plants may be transplanted in autumn either from the garden or from the bed of summer cuttings just mentioned, kept in a rather cool temperature during the winter and drawn upon for cuttings as the stems become sufficiently mature. The rooting may take place in a regular cutting bench, or it may occur in the soil out of doors, the plantlets being transplanted to pots as soon as they have rooted well.

If a large number of plants is desired, a hotbed may be called into requisition in early spring and the plants hardened off in cold frames as the season advances. Hardening off is essential with all plants grown under glass for outdoor planting, because unless the plants be inured to outside temperatures before being placed in the open ground, they will probably suffer a check, if they do not succumb wholly to the unaccustomed conditions. If well managed they should be injured not at all.

LAYERS

Several of the perennial herbs, such as sage, savory, and thyme, may be easily propagated by means of layers, the stems being pegged down and covered lightly with earth. If the moisture and the temperature be favorable, roots should be formed in three or four weeks and the stem separated from the parent and planted. Often there may be several branches upon the stem, and each of these may be used as a new plantlet provided it has some roots or a rooted part of the main stem attached to it. By this method I have obtained nearly 100 rooted plants from a single specimen of Holt's Mammoth sage grown in a greenhouse. And from the same plant at the same time I have taken more than 100 cuttings. This is not an exceptional feat with this variety, the plants of which are very branchy and often exceed a yard in diameter.

Layering is probably the simplest and most satisfactory method of artificial propagation under ordinary conditions, since the stems are almost sure to take root if undisturbed long enough; and since rooted plants can hardly fail to grow if properly transplanted. Then, too, less apparent time is taken than with plants grown from cuttings and far less than with those grown from seed. In other words, they generally produce a crop sooner than the plants obtained by the other methods set in operation at the same time.

DIVISION

Division of the clumps of such herbs as mint is often practiced, a sharp spade or a lawn edger being used to cut the clump into pieces about 6 inches square. The squares are then placed in new quarters and packed firmly in place with soil. This method is, however, the least satisfactory of all mentioned, because it too frequently deprives the plants of a large amount of roots, thus impairs the growth, and during the first season or two may result in unsymmetrical clumps. If done in early spring before growth starts, least damage is done to the plants.

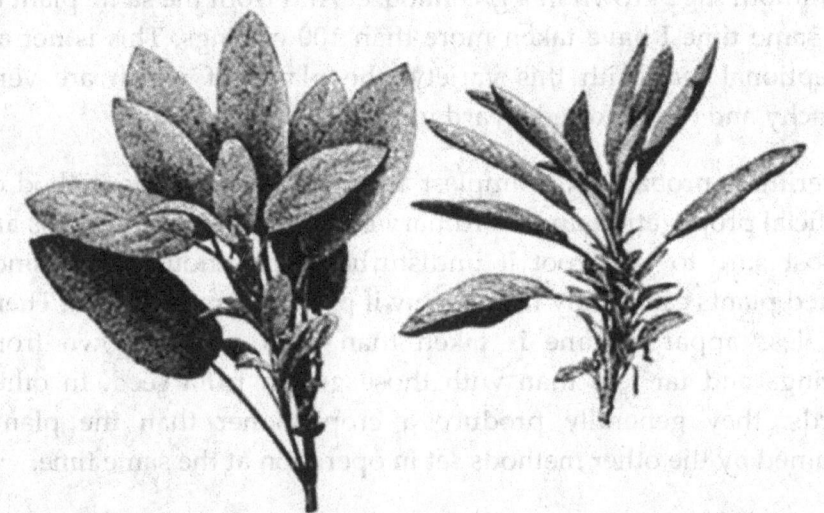

Holt's Mammoth and Common Sage About Half Natural Size

Artificial methods of propagation, especially those of cuttage and layerage, have the further advantage over propagation by means of seeds, in the perpetuation of desired characters of individual plants, one or more of which may appear in any plantation. These, particularly if more productive than the others, should always be utilized as stock, not merely because their progeny artificially obtained are likely to retain the character and thus probably increase the yield of the plantation, but principally because they may form the nucleus of a choice strain.

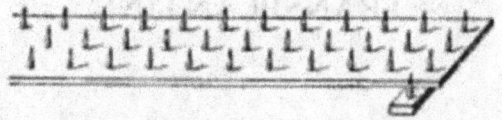

Marker for Hotbeds and Cold Frames

Except in the respects mentioned, these methods of propagation are not notably superior to propagation by means of good seed, which, by the way, is not overabundant. By the consumption of a little extra time, any desired number of plants may be obtained from seed. At any rate, seed is what one must start with in nearly every case.

TRANSPLANTING

No more care is required in transplanting herbs than in resetting other plants, but unless a few essentials are realized in practice the results are sure to be unsatisfactory. Of course, the ideal way is to grow the plants in small flower pots and when they have formed a ball of roots, to set them in the garden. The next best is to grow them in seed pans or flats (shallow boxes) in which they should be set several inches apart as soon as large enough to handle, and in which they should be allowed to grow for a few weeks, to form a mass of roots. When these plants are to be set in the garden they should be broken apart by hand with as little loss of roots as possible.

Leading Forms of Trowels

But where neither of these plans can be practiced, as in the growing of the plants in little nursery beds, either in hotbeds, cold frames or in the garden border, the plants should be "pricked out," that is, transplanted while very small to a second nursery bed, in order to make them "stocky" or sturdy and better able to take care of themselves when removed to final quarters. If this be done there should be no need of clipping back the tops to balance an excessive loss of roots, a necessity in case the plants are not so treated, or in case they become large or lanky in the second bed.

In all cases it is best to transplant when the ground is moist, as it is immediately after being dug or plowed. But this cannot always be arranged, neither can one always count upon a shower to moisten the soil just after the plants have been set. If advantage can be taken of an approaching rainfall, it should be done, because this is the ideal time for transplanting. It is much better than immediately after, which is perhaps next best. Transplanting in cloudy weather and toward evening is better than in sunny weather and in the morning.

Since the weather is prone to be coy, if not fickle, the manual part of transplanting should always be properly done. The plants should always be taken up with as little loss of roots as possible, be kept exposed to the air as short a time as possible, and when set in the ground have the soil packed firmly about their roots, so firmly that the operator may think it is almost too firm. After setting, the surface soil should be made loose, so as to act as a mulch and prevent the loss of moisture from the packed lower layer. If the ground be dry a hole may be made beside the plant and filled with water—LOTS OF WATER—and when it has soaked away and the soil seems to be drying, the surface should be made smooth and loose as already mentioned. If possible such times should be avoided, because of the extra work entailed and the probable increased loss due to the unfavorable conditions.

IMPLEMENTS

When herbs are grown upon a commercial scale the implements needed will be the same as for general trucking—plows, harrows, weeder, etc.—to fit the soil for the hand tools. Much labor can be saved by using hand-wheel drills, cultivators, weeders and the other tools that have become so wonderfully popular within the past decade or two. Some typical kinds are shown in these pages. These implements are indispensable in keeping the surface soil loose and free from weeds, especially between the rows and even fairly close to the plants. In doing this they save an immense amount of labor and time, since they can be used with both hands and the muscles of the body with less exertion than the hoe and the rake require.

Nothing, however, can take the place of the hand tools for getting among and around the plants. The work that weeding entails is tiresome, but must be done if success is to crown ones efforts. While the plants are little some of the weeders may be used. Those with a blade or a series of blades are adapted for cutting weeds off close to the surface; those with prongs are useful only for making the soil loose closer to the plants than the rake dare be run by the average man. Hoes of various types are useful when the plants become somewhat larger or when one does not have the wheel cultivators. In all well-regulated gardens there should be a little liberal selection of the various wheel and hand tools.

Only one of the hand tools demands any special comment. Many gardeners like to use a dibble for transplanting. With this tool it is so easy to make a hole, and to press the soil against the plant dropped in that hole! But I believe that many of the failures in transplanting result from the improper use of this tool. Unless the dibble be properly operated the plant may be left suspended in a hole, the sides of which are more or less hard and impervious to the tiny, tender rootlets that strive to penetrate them. From my own observation of the use of this tool, I believe that the proper place for the dibble in the novices garden is in the attic, side by side with the "unloaded" shotgun, where it may be viewed with apprehension.

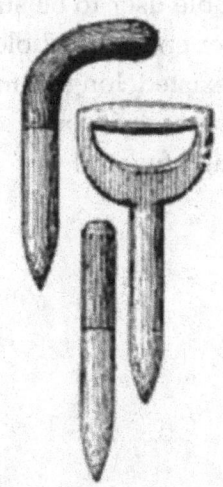

Wooden Dibbles

In spite of this warning, if anyone is hardy enough to use a dibble, let him choose the flat style, not the round one. The proper way is to thrust the tool straight down, at right angles to the direction of the row, and press the soil back and forth with the flat side of the blade until a hole, say 2 or 3 inches across and 5 or 6 inches deep, has been formed. In the hole the plantlet should then be suspended so all the roots and a little of the stem beneath the surface will be covered when the soil is replaced. Replacing the soil is the important part of the operation. The dibble must now be thrust in the soil again, parallel and close to the hole, and the soil pushed over so the hole will be completely closed from bottom to top. Firming the soil completes the operation.

There is much less danger of leaving a hole with the flat than with the round dibble, which is almost sure to leave a hole beneath the plant. I remember having trouble with some lily plants which were not thriving. Supposing that insects were at the roots, I carefully drew the earth away from one side, and found that the earth had not been brought up carefully beneath the bulbs and that the roots were hanging 4 or 5 inches beneath the bulbs in the hole left by the dibble and not properly closed by the careless gardener.

I therefore warn every dibble user to be sure to crowd over the soil well, especially at the lower end of the hole. For my own part, I rely upon my hands. Digits existed long before dibbles and they are much more reliable. What matter if some soil sticks to them; it is not unresponsive to the wooing of water!

LOCATION OF HERB GARDEN

In general, the most favorable exposure for an herb garden is toward the south, but lacking such an exposure should not deter one from planting herbs on a northern slope if this be the only site available. Indeed, such sites often prove remarkably good if other conditions are propitious and proper attention is given the plants. Similarly, a smooth, gently sloping surface is especially desirable, but even in gardens in which the ground is almost billowy the gardener may often take advantage of the irregularities by planting the moisture-loving plants in the hollows and those that like dry situations upon the ridges. Nothing like turning disadvantages to account!

No matter what the nature of the surface and the exposure, it is always advisable to give the herbs the most sunny spots in the garden, places where shade from trees, barns, other buildings and from fences cannot reach them. This is suggested because the development of the oils, upon which the flavoring of most of the herbs mainly depends, is best in full sunshine and the plants have more substance than when grown in the shade.

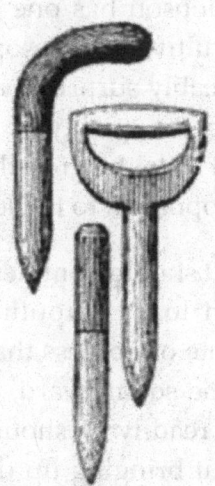

Combination Hand Plow, Harrow, Cultivator and Seed Drill

THE SOIL AND ITS PREPARATION

As to the kind of soil, Hobson's choice ranks first! It is not necessary to move into the next county just to have an herb garden. This is one of the cases in which the gardener may well make the best of however bad a bargain he has.

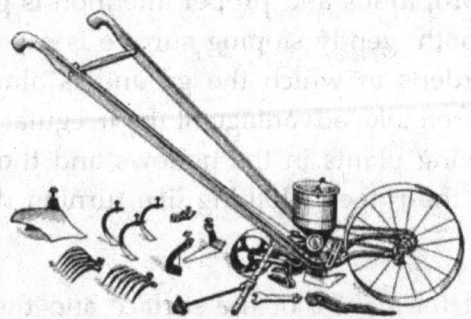

Combination Hand Plow, Harrow, Cultivator and Seed Drill

But supposing that a selection be possible, a light sandy loam, underlaid by a porous subsoil so as to be well drained, should be given the preference, since it is warmed quickly, easily worked, and may be stirred early in the season and after a rain. Clay loams are less desirable upon every one of the points mentioned, and very sandy soils also. But if Hobson has one of these, there will be an excellent opportunity to cultivate philosophy as well as herbs. And the gardener may be agreeably surprised at the results obtained. No harm in trying! Whatever the quality of the soil, it should not be very rich, because in such soils the growth is apt to be rank and the quantity of oil small in proportion to the leafage.

The preparation of the soil should commence as soon as the grass in the neighborhood is seen to be sprouting. Well-decayed manure should be spread at the rate of not less than a bushel nor more than double that quantity to the square yard, and as soon as the soil is dry enough to crumble readily it should be dug or plowed as deeply as possible without bringing up the subsoil. This operation of turning over the soil should be thoroughly performed, the earth being pulverized as much as possible. To accomplish this no hand tool surpasses the spading fork.

Surface Paring Cultivator

One other method is, however, superior especially when practiced upon the heavier soils—fall plowing or digging. In practicing this method care should be taken to plow late when the soil, moistened by autumn rains, will naturally come up in big lumps. These lumps must be left undisturbed during the winter for frost to act upon. All that will be necessary in the spring will be to rake or harrow the ground. The clods will crumble.

I once had occasion to try this method upon about 25 acres of land which had been made by pumping mud from a river bottom upon a marsh thus converted into dry ground by the sedimentation. Three sturdy horses were needed to do the plowing. The earth turned up in chunks as large as a man's body. Contrary to my plowman's doubts and predictions, Jack Frost did a grand milling business that winter! Clods that could hardly be broken in the autumn with a sledge hammer crumbled down in the spring at the touch of a garden rake!

CULTIVATION

Having thoroughly fined the surface of the garden by harrowing and raking, the seeds may be sown or the plants transplanted as already noted. From this time forward the surface must be kept loose and open by surface cultivation every week or 10 days and after every shower that forms a crust, until the plants cover the whole ground. This frequent cultivation is not merely for the purpose of keeping the weeds in check; it is a necessary operation to keep the immediate surface layer powdery, in which condition it will act as a mulch to prevent the loss of water from the lower soil layers. When kept in perfect condition by frequent stirring the immediate surface should be powdery. Yes, *powdery*! Within 1 inch of the surface, however, the color will be darker from the presence of moisture. When supplied with such conditions, failures must be attributed to other causes than lack of water.

DOUBLE CROPPING

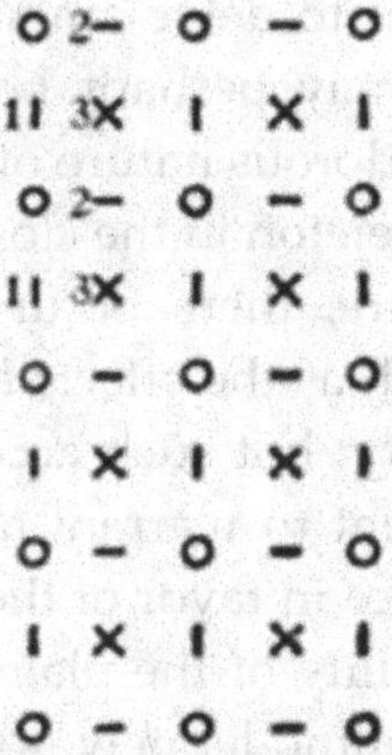

```
O 2-  O  -  O
II 3X  I  X  I
O 2-  O  -  O
II 3X  I  X  I
O  -  O  -  O
I  X  I  X  I
O  -  O  -  O
I  X  I  X  I
O  -  O  -  O
```

**Thinning Scheme
for Harvesting**

When desired, herbs may be used as secondary crops to follow such early vegetables as early cabbage and peas; or, if likely to be needed still earlier, after radishes, transplanted lettuce and onions grown from sets. These primary crops, having reached marketable size, are removed, the ground stirred and the herb plants transplanted from nursery beds or cold frames.

Often the principal herbs—sage, savory, marjoram and thyme—are set close together, both the rows and the plants in them being nearer than recommended further on. The object of such practice is to get several crops in the following way: When the plants in the rows commence to crowd one another each alternate plant is removed and sold or cured. This may perhaps be done a second time. Then when the rows begin to crowd, each alternate row is removed and the remainder allowed to develop more fully. The chief advantages of this practice are not only that several crops may be gathered, but each plant, being supplied with plenty of room and light, will have fewer yellow or dead leaves than when crowded. In the diagram the numbers show which plants are removed first, second, third and last.

HERB RELATIONSHIPS

Those readers who delight to delve among pedigrees, genealogies and family connections, may perhaps be a little disappointed to learn that, in spite of the odorous nature of the herbs, there are none whose history reveals a skeleton in the closet. They are all harmless. Now and then, to be sure, there occur records of a seemingly compromising nature, such as the effects attributed to the eating or even the handling of celery; but such accounts, harrowing as they may appear, are insufficient to warrant a bar sinister. Indeed, not only is the mass of evidence in favor of the defendant, but it casts a reflection upon the credibility of the plaintiff, who may usually be shown to have indulged immoderately, to have been frightened by hallucinations or even to have arraigned the innocent for his own guilt. Certain it is that there is not one of the sweet herbs mentioned in this volumes that has not long enjoyed a more or less honored place in the cuisine of all the continents, and this in spite of the occasional tootings of some would-be detractor.

Like those classes of society that cannot move with "the four hundred," the herbs are very exclusive, more exclusive indeed, than their superiors, the other vegetables. Very few members have they admitted that do not belong to two approved families, and such unrelated ones as do reach the charmed circles must first prove their worthiness and then hold their places by intrinsic merit.

**Center Row
Hand Cultivator**

These two coteries are known as the Labiatæ and the Umbelliferæ, the former including the sages, mints and their connections; the latter the parsleys and their relatives. With the exception of tarragon, which belongs to the Compositæ, parsley and a few of its relatives which have deserted their own ranks, all the important leaf herbs belong to the Labiatæ; and without a notable exception all the herbs whose seeds are used for flavoring belong to the Umbelliferæ. Fennel-flower, which belongs to the natural order Ranunculaceæ, or crowfoot family, is a candidate for admission to the seed sodality; costmary and southernwood of the Compositæ seek membership with the leaf faction; rue of the Rutaceæ and tansy of the Compositæ, in spite of suspension for their boldness and ill-breeding, occasionally force their way back into the domain of the leaf herbs. Marigold, a composite, forms a clique by itself, the most exclusive club of all. It has admitted no members! And there seem to be no candidates.

The important members of the Labiatæ are:

Sage (*Salvia officinalis, Linn.*).
Savory (*Satureia hortensis, Linn.*).
Savory, winter (*Satureia montana, Linn.*).
Thyme (*Thymus vulgaris, Linn.*).
Marjoram (*Origanum Marjoram; O. Onites, Linn.; and M. vulgare, Linn.*).
Balm (*Melissa officinalis, Linn.*).
Basil (*Ocimum Basilicum, Linn., and O. minimum, Linn.*).
Spearmint (*Mentha spicata, Linn., or M. viridis, Linn.*).
Peppermint (*Mentha Piperita, Linn.*).
Rosemary (*Rosmarinus officinalis, Linn.*).
Clary (*Salvia Sclarea, Linn.*).
Pennyroyal (*Mentha Pulegium, Linn.*).
Horehound (*Marrubium vulgare, Linn.*).
Hyssop (*Hyssopus vulgaris, Linn.*).
Catnip (*Nepeta Cataria, Linn.*).
Lavender (*Lavandula vera, D. C.; L. spica, D. C.*).

These plants, which are mostly natives of mild climates of the old world, are characterized by having square stems; opposite, simple leaves and branches; and more or less two-lipped flowers which appear in the axils of the leaves, occasionally alone, but usually several together, forming little whorls, which often compose loose or compact spikes or racemes. Each fertile blossom is followed by four little seedlike fruits in the bottom of the calyx, which remains attached to the plant. The foliage is generally plentifully dotted with minute glands that contain a volatile oil, upon which depends the aroma and piquancy peculiar to the individual species.

The leading species of the Umbelliferæ are:

> Parsley (*Carum Petroselinum, Benth. and Hook.*).
> Dill (*Anethum graveolens, Linn.*).
> Fennel (*Fœniculum officinale, Linn.*).
> Angelica (*Archangelica officinalis, Hoofm.*).
> Anise (*Pimpinella anisum, Linn.*).
> Caraway (*Carum Carui, Linn.*).
> Coriander (*Coriandrum sativum, Linn.*).
> Chervil (*Scandix Cerefolium, Linn.*).
> Cumin or Cummin (*Cuminum Cyminum, Linn.*).
> Lovage (*Levisticum officinale, Koch.*).
> Samphire (*Crithmum maritimum, Linn.*).

Hand Plow

Like the members of the preceding group, the species of the Umbelliferæ are principally natives of mild climates of the old world, but many of them extend farther north into the cold parts of the continent, even beyond the Arctic Circle in some cases. They have cylindrical, usually hollow stems; alternate, generally compound leaves the basis of whose stalks ensheath the branches or stems; and small flowers almost always arranged in compound terminal umbels. The fruits are composed of two seedlike dry carpels, each containing a single seed, and usually separating when ripe. Each carpel bears five longitudinal prominent ribs and several, often four, lesser intermediate ones, in the intervals between which numerous oil ducts have their openings from the interior of the fruit. The oil is generally found in more or less abundance also in other parts of the plant, but is usually most plentiful in the fruits.

The members of the Compositæ used as sweet herbs are, with the exception of tarragon, comparatively unimportant, and except for having their flowers in close heads "on a common receptacle, surrounded by an involucre," have few conspicuous characters in common. No further space except that required for their enumeration need here be devoted to them. And this remark will apply also to the other two herbs mentioned further below.

COMPOSITÆ

Marigold, Pot (*Calendula officinalis*, Linn.). Tansy (*Tanacetum vulgaris*, Linn.). Tarragon (*Artemisia Dracunculus*, Linn.). Southernwood (*Artemisia Abrotanum*, Linn.).

RUTACEÆ

Rue (*Ruta graveolens*, Linn.).

BORAGINACEÆ

Borage (*Borago officinalis*, Linn.).

RANUNCULACEÆ

Fennel-flower (*Nigella sativa*, Linn.).

Before dismissing this section of the subject, it may be interesting to glance over the list of names once more. Seven of these plants were formerly so prominent in medicine that they were designated "official" and nearly all the others were extensively used by physicians. At the present day there are very few that have not passed entirely out of official medicine and even out of domestic practice, at least so far as their intrinsic qualities are concerned. Some, to be sure, are still employed because of their pleasant flavors, which disguise the disagreeable taste of other drugs. But this is a very different matter.

One of the most notable of these is fennel. What wonders could that plant not perform 300 years ago! In Parkinson's "Theatricum Botanicum" (1640) its "vertues" are recorded. Apart from its use as food, for which, then, as now, it was highly esteemed, without the attachment of any medicinal qualities as an esculent, it was considered efficacious in cases of gout, jaundice, cramps, shortness of breath, wheezing of the lungs; for cleansing of the blood and improving the complexion; to use as an eye-water or to increase the flow of milk; as a remedy for serpent bites or an antidote for poisonous herbs and mushrooms; and for people who "are growen fat to abate their unwieldinesse and make them more gaunt and lanke."

But let us peep into the 19th edition of the United States Dispensatory. Can this be the same fennel which "is one of our most grateful aromatics," and which, because of "the absence of any highly excitant property," is recommended for mixing with unpleasant medicines? Ask any druggist, and he will say it is used for little else nowadays than for making a tea to give babies for wind on their stomachs. Strange, but true it is! Similar statements if not more remarkable ones could be made about many of the other herbs herein discussed. Many of these are spoken of as "formerly considered specific" for such and such troubles but "now known to be inert."

The cause is not far to seek. An imaginative and superstitious people attached fanciful powers to these and hundreds of other plants which the intervening centuries have been unable wholly to eradicate, for among the more ignorant classes, especially of Europe, many of these relics of a dark age still persist.

But let us not gloat over our superior knowledge. After a similar lapse of time, may not our vaunted wisdom concerning the properties of plants look as ridiculous to the delver among our musty volumes? Indeed, it may, if we may judge by the discoveries and investigations of only the past fifty years. During this time a surprisingly large number of plants have been proved to be not merely innocuous instead of poisonous, as they were reputed, but fit for human food and even of superior excellence!

THE HERB LIST

Angelica (*Archangelica officinalis*, Hoffm.), a biennial or perennial herb of the natural order Umbelliferæ, so called from its supposed medicinal qualities. It is believed to be a native of Syria, from whence it has spread to many cool European climates, especially Lapland and the Alps, where it has become naturalized.

Prophecy of Many Toothsome Dishes

Description. Its roots are long, spindle-shaped, fleshy, and sometimes weigh three pounds; its stems stout, herbaceous, fluted, often more than 4 feet tall, and hollow; its leaves long-stalked, frequently 3 feet in length, reddish purple at the clasping bases, and composed, in the larger ones, of numerous small leaflets, in three principal groups, which are each subdivided into three lesser groups; its flowers yellowish or greenish, small and numerous, in large roundish umbels; its seeds pale yellow, membranous-edged, oblong flattened on one side, convex on the other, which is marked with three conspicuous ribs.

Cultivation. Since the seeds lose their vitality rapidly, rarely being viable after the first year, they should be sown as soon as ripe in late summer or early autumn, or not later than the following spring after having been kept during the winter in a cold storeroom. The soil should be moderately rich, rather light, deep, well drained, but moist and well supplied with humus. It should be deeply prepared and kept loose and open as long as tools can be used among the plants, which may be left to care for themselves as soon as they shade the ground well.

In the autumn, the seeds may be sown where the plants are to remain or preferably in a nursery bed, which usually does not need protection during the winter. In the spring a mild hotbed, a cold frame or a nursery bed in the garden may be used, according to the earliness of planting. Half an inch is deep enough to cover the seeds. The seedlings should be transplanted when still small for their first summer's growth, a space of about 18 inches being allowed between them. In the autumn they should be removed to permanent quarters, the plants being set 3 feet apart.

If well grown, the leaves may be cut for use during the summer after transplanting; the plants may not, however, produce seed until the following season. Unless seed is desired, the tops should be cut and destroyed at or before flowering time, because, if this be not done, the garden is apt to become overrun with angelica seedlings. If the seeds are wanted, they should be gathered and treated as indicated on **page 24**. After producing seed, the plants frequently die; but by cutting down the tops when the flower heads first appear, and thus preventing the formation of seed, the plants may continue for several years longer.

Uses. The stems and leaf stalks, while still succulent, are eaten as a salad or are roasted or boiled like potatoes. In Europe, they are frequently employed as a garnish or as an adjunct to dishes of meat and fish. They are also largely used for making candied angelica. (See below.) Formerly the stems were blanched like celery and were very popular as a vegetable; now they are little used in the United States. The tender leaves are often boiled and eaten as a substitute for spinach. Less in America than in Europe, the seeds, which, like other parts of the plant, are aromatic and bitterish, are used for flavoring various beverages, cakes, and candies, especially "comfits." Oil of angelica is obtained from the seeds by distillation with steam or boiling water, the vapor being condensed and the oil separated by gravity. It is also obtained in smaller quantity from the roots, 200 pounds of which, it is said, yield only about one pound of the oil. Like the seeds, the oil is used for flavoring.

Angelica candied. Green says: The fresh roots, the tender stems, the leaf stalks and the midribs of the leaves make a pleasing aromatic candy. When fresh gathered the plant is rather too bitter for use. This flavor may be reduced by boiling. The parts should first be sliced lengthwise, to remove the pith. The length of time will depend somewhat upon the thickness of the pieces. A few minutes is usually sufficient. After removal and draining the pieces are put in a syrup of granulated sugar and boiled till full candy density is reached. The kettle is then removed from the fire and the contents allowed to cool. When almost cold the pieces are to be taken out and allowed to dry.

Anise (*Pimpinella Anisum*, Linn.), an annual herb of the natural order Umbelliferæ. It is a native of southwestern Asia, northern Africa and south-eastern Europe, whence it has been introduced by man throughout the Mediterranean region, into Germany, and to some extent into other temperate regions of both hemispheres, but seems not to be known anywhere in the wild state or as an escape from gardens. To judge from its mention in the Scriptures (Matthew xxiii, 23), it was highly valued as a cultivated crop prior to our era, not only in Palestine, but elsewhere in the East. Many Greek and

Roman authors, especially Dioscorides, Theophrastus, Pliny and Paladius, wrote more or less fully of its cultivation and uses.

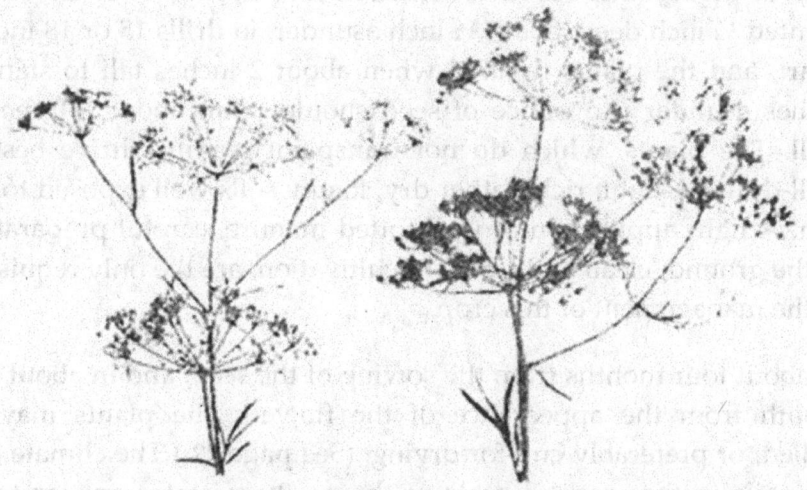

Anise in Flower and in Fruit

From their days to the present it seems to have enjoyed general popularity. In the ninth century, Charlemagne commanded that it be grown upon the imperial farms; in the thirteenth, Albertus Magnus speaks highly of it; and since then many agricultural writers have devoted attention to it. But though it has been cultivated for at least two thousand years and is now extensively grown in Malta, Spain, southern France, Russia, Germany and India, which mainly supply the market, it seems not to have developed any improved varieties.

Description.—Its roots are white, spindle-shaped and rather fibrous; its stems about 18 inches tall, branchy, erect, slender, cylindrical; its root leaves lobed somewhat like those of celery; its stem leaves more and more finely cut toward the upper part of the stem, near the top of which they resemble fennel leaves in their finely divided segments; its flowers yellowish white, small, rather large, in loose umbels consisting of many umbellets; its fruits ("seeds") greenish-gray, small, ovoid or oblong in outline, longitudinally furrowed and ridged on the convex side, very aromatic, sweetish and pleasantly piquant.

Cultivation.—The seeds, which should be as fresh as possible, never more than two years old, should be sown in permanent quarters as soon as the weather becomes settled in early spring. They should be planted ½ inch deep, about ½ inch asunder, in drills 15 or 18 inches apart, and the plants thinned when about 2 inches tall to stand 6 inches asunder. An ounce of seed should plant about 150 feet of drill. The plants, which do not transplant readily, thrive best in well-drained, light, rich, rather dry, loamy soils well exposed to the sun. A light application of well-rotted manure, careful preparation of the ground, clean and frequent cultivation, are the only requisites in the management of this crop.

In about four months from the sowing of the seed, and in about one month from the appearance of the flowers, the plants may be pulled, or preferably cut, for drying. (See **page 22**.) The climate and the soils in the warmer parts of the northern states appear to be favorable to the commercial cultivation of anise, which it seems should prove a profitable crop under proper management.

Uses.—The leaves are frequently employed as a garnish, for flavoring salads, and to a small extent as potherbs. Far more general, however, is the use of the seeds, which enter as a flavoring into various condiments, especially curry powders, many kinds of cake, pastry, and confectionery and into some kinds of cheese and bread. Anise oil is extensively employed for flavoring many beverages both alcoholic and non-spirituous and for disguising the unpleasant flavors of various drugs. The seeds are also ground and compounded with other fragrant materials for making sachet powders, and the oil mixed with other fluids for liquid perfumes. Various similar anise combinations are largely used in perfuming soaps, pomatums and other toilet articles. The very volatile, nearly colorless oil is usually obtained by distillation with water, about 50 pounds of seed being required to produce one pound of oil. At Erfurt, Germany, where much of the commercial oil is made, the "hay" and the seeds are both used for distilling.

Balm (*Melissa officinalis*, Linn.), a perennial herb of the natural order

Labiatæ. The popular name is a contraction of *balsam*, the plant having formerly been considered a specific for a host of ailments. The generic name, *Melissa*, is the Greek for *bee* and is an allusion to the fondness of bees for the abundant nectar of the flowers.

Balm is a native of southern Europe, where it was cultivated as a source of honey and as a sweet herb more than 2,000 years ago. It is frequently mentioned in Greek and Latin poetry and prose. Because of its use for anointing, Shakespeare referred to it in the glorious lines (King Richard II., act iii, scene 2):

"Not all the water in the rough, rude sea
Can wash the balm from an anointed king."

As a useful plant it received attention from the pen of Pliny. From its home it has been introduced by man as a garden plant into nearly all temperate climates throughout the world, and is often found as an escape from gardens where introduced—occasionally in this role in the earliest settled of the United States. Very few well-marked varieties have been produced. A variegated one, now grown for ornament as well as for culinary purposes, is probably the same as that mentioned by Mawe in 1778.

Description.—The roots are small and fibrous; the stems, about 18 inches tall, very numerous, erect or spreading, square; the leaves, green (except as mentioned), broadly ovate with toothed margins, opposite, rather succulent, highly scented; the flowers, few, whitish, or purplish, in small, loose, axillary, one-sided clusters borne from midsummer until late autumn; the seeds very small—more than 50,000 to the ounce.

Cultivation.—Balm is readily propagated by means of divisions, layers, cuttings, and by its seeds, which germinate fairly well even when four years old. Owing to its small size, the seed should be planted in a seedpan or flat in a greenhouse or hotbed, where all conditions can be controlled. The soil should be made very fine and friable, the thinly scattered seeds merely pressed upon the surface with a block or a brick, and water applied preferably through the bottom of the seedpan, which may be set in a shallow dish of water until the surface of the soil *begins* to appear moist.

When an inch tall the seedlings should be pricked out 2 inches apart in other, deeper flats and when about 4 inches tall set in the garden about 1 foot asunder in rows about 18 inches apart. When once established they may be increased readily by the artificial means mentioned. (See **page 30**.) Ordinary clean cultivation throughout the season, the removal of dead parts, and care to prevent the plants from spreading unduly, are the only requisites of cultivation. Preferably the soil should be poor, rather dry, little if at all enriched and in a sunny place. The foliage of seedling plants or plants newly spring-set should be ready for use by midsummer; that of established plants from early spring until late autumn. For home use and market it should be cured as recommended on **page 22**, the leaves being very thinly spread and plentifully supplied with air because of their succulence. The temperature should be rather low.

Uses.—The foliage is widely used for flavoring soups, stews, sauces, and dressings, and, when fresh, to a small extent with salads. Otto or oil of balm, obtained by aqueous distillation from the "hay," is a pale yellow, essential and volatile oil highly prized in perfumery for its lemon-like odor, and is extensively employed for flavoring various beverages.

Basil (*Ocymum basilicum*, Linn.), an annual herb of the order Labiatæ. The popular name, derived from the specific, signifies royal or kingly, probably because of the plant's use in feasts. In France it is known as herb royale, royal herb. The generic name is derived from *Oza*, a Greek word signifying odor.

The plant is a native of tropical Asia, where for centuries, especially in India, it has been highly esteemed as a condiment. Probably the early Greek and Roman writers were well acquainted with it, but commentators are not decided. They suppose that the *Okimon* of Hippocrates, Dioscorides and Theophrastus is the same as *Ocimum hortense* of Columella and Varro.

Sweet Basil

The plant's introduction into England was about 1548, or perhaps a little earlier, but probably not prior to 1538, because Turner does not mention it in his "Libellus," published in that year. It seems to have grown rapidly in popularity, for in 1586 Lyte speaks of it as if well known. In America it has been cultivated somewhat for about a century partly because of its fragrant leaves which are employed in bouquets, but mainly for flavoring culinary concoctions. In Australia it is also more or less grown, and in countries where French commerce or other interests have penetrated it is well known.

There are several related species which, in America less than in Europe or the East, have attracted attention. The most important of these is dwarf or bush basil (*O. minimum*, Linn.), a small Chilian species also reported from Cochin China. It was introduced into cultivation in Europe in 1573. On account of its compact form it is popular in gardens as an edging as well as a culinary herb, for more than a century it has been grown in America. Sacred basil (*O. sanctum*), an oriental species, is cultivated near temples in India and its odoriferous oil extracted for religious uses. Formerly the common species was considered sacred by the Brahmins who used it especially in honor of Vishnu and in funeral rites. An African species, *O. fruticosum*, is highly valued at the Cape of Good Hope for its perfume.

Description.—From the small, fibrous roots the square stems stand erect about 1 foot tall. They are very branching and leafy. The leaves are green, except as noted below, ovate, pointed, opposite, somewhat toothed, rather succulent and highly fragrant. The little white flowers which appear in midsummer are racemed in leafy whorls, followed by small black fruits, popularly called seeds. These, like flaxseed, emit a mucilaginous substance when soaked in water. About 23,000 weigh an ounce, and 10 ounces fill a pint. Their vitality lasts about eight years.

Like most of the other culinary herbs, basil has varied little in several centuries; there are no well-marked varieties of modern origin. Only three varieties of common basil are listed in America; Vilmorin lists only five French ones. Purple basil has lilac flowers, and when grown in the sun also purple leaf stems and young branches. Lettuce-leaved basil has large, pale-green blistered and wrinkled leaves like those of lettuce. Its closely set clusters of flowers appear somewhat late. The leaves are larger and fewer than in the common variety.

The dwarf species is more compact, branching and dainty than the common species. It has three varieties; one with deep violet foliage and stems and lilac white flowers, and two with green leaves, one very dense and compact.

East Indian, or Tree Basil (*O. gratissimum*, Linn.), a well-known species in the Orient, seems to have a substitute in *O. suave*, also known by the same popular name, and presumably the species cultivated in Europe and to some extent in America. It is an upright, branching annual, which forms a pyramidal bush about 20 inches tall and often 15 inches in diameter. It favors very warm situations and tropical countries.

Cultivation.—Basil is propagated by seeds. Because these are very small, they are best sown in flats under glass, covered lightly with finely sifted soil and moistened by standing in a shallow pan of water until the surface shows a wet spot. When about an inch tall, the seedlings must be pricked out 2 inches apart each way in larger-sized flats. When 3 inches tall they will be large enough for the garden, where they should be set 1 foot asunder in rows 15 to 18 inches apart. Often the seed is sown in the mellow border as early in the spring as the ground can be worked. This method demands perhaps more attention than the former, because of weeds and because the rows cannot be easily seen. When transplanting, preference should be given to a sunny situation in a mellow, light, fertile, rather dry soil thoroughly well prepared and as free from weeds as possible. From the start the ground must be kept loose, open and clean. When the plants meet in the rows cultivation may stop.

First gatherings of foliage should begin by midsummer when the plants start to blossom. Then they may be cut to within a few inches of the ground. The stumps should develop a second and even a third crop if care is exercised to keep the surface clean and open. A little dressing of quickly available fertilizer applied at this time is helpful. For seed some of the best plants should be left uncut. The seed should ripen by mid-autumn.

For winter use plants may be transplanted from the garden, or seedlings may be started in September. The seeds should be sown two to the inch and the seedlings transplanted to pots or boxes. A handy pot is the 4-inch standard; this is large enough for one plant. In flats the plants should be 5 or 6 inches apart each way.

Uses.—Basil is one of the most popular herbs in the French cuisine. It is especially relished in mock turtle soup, which, when correctly made, derives its peculiar taste chiefly from the clovelike flavor of basil. In other highly seasoned dishes, such as stews and dressings, basil is also highly prized. It is less used in salads. A golden yellow essential oil, which reddens with age, is extracted from the leaves for uses in perfumery more than in the kitchen.

The original and famous Fetter Lane sausages, formerly popular with Cockney epicures, owed their reputation mainly to basil.

During the reigns of Queen Mary and Queen Elizabeth farmers grew basil in pots and presented them with compliments to their landladies when these paid their visits.

Borage, Famous for "Cool Tankard"

Borage (*Borago officinalis*, Linn.), a coarse, hardy, annual herb of the natural order Boraginaceæ. Its popular name, derived from the generic, is supposed by some to have come from a corruption of *cor*, the heart, and *ago*, to affect, because of its former use as a cordial or heart-fortifying medicine. *Courage* is from the same source. The Standard Dictionary, however, points to *burrago*, rough, and relates it indirectly by cross references to *birrus*, a thick, coarse woolen cloth worn by the poor during the thirteenth century. The roughness of the full-grown leaves suggests flannel. Whichever derivation be correct, each is interesting as implying qualities, intrinsic or attributed, to the plant.

The specific name indicates its obsolete use in medicine. It is one of the numerous plants which have shaken off the superstitions which a credulous populace wreathed around them. Almost none but the least enlightened people now attribute any medicinal virtues whatever to it.

The plant is said to come originally from Aleppo, but for centuries has been considered a native of Mediterranean Europe and Africa, whence it has become naturalized throughout the world by Europeans, who grew it probably more for medicinal than for culinary purposes. According to Ainslie, it was among the species listed by Peter Martyr as planted on Isabella Island by Columbus's companions. The probability is that it was also brought to America by the colonists during Queen Elizabeth's time. It has been listed in American seedsmen's catalogues since 1806, but the demand has always been small and the extent to which it is cultivated very limited.

Description.—Borage is of somewhat spreading habit, branchy, about 20 inches tall. Its oval or oblong-lanceolate leaves and other green parts are covered with whitish, rather sharp, spreading hairs. The flowers, generally blue, sometimes pink, violet-red, or white, are loosely racemed at the extremities of the branches and main stems.

> "The flaming rose glooms swarthy red;
> The borage gleams more blue;
> And low white flowers, with starry head,
> Glimmer the rich dusk through."
>
> —*George MacDonald*
> *"Songs of the Summer Night," Part III*

The seeds are rather large, oblong, slightly curved, and a ridged and streaked grayish-brown. They retain their vitality for about eight years.

Cultivation.—No plant is more easily grown. The seed need only be dropped and covered in any soil, from poor to rich, and the plants will grow like weeds, and even become such if allowed to have sway. Borage seems, however, to prefer rather light, dry soils, waste places and steep banks. Upon such the flavor of the flowers is declared to be superior to that produced upon richer ground, which develops a ranker growth of foliage.

In the garden the seeds are sown about ½ inch asunder and in rows 15 inches apart. Shortly after the plants appear they are thinned to stand 3 inches apart, the thinnings being cooked like spinach, or, if small and delicate, they may be made into salads. Two other thinnings may be given for similar purposes as the plants grow, so that at the final thinning the specimens will stand about a foot asunder. Up to this time the ground is kept open and clean by cultivation; afterwards the borage will usually have possession.

Uses.—More popular than the use of the foliage as a potherb and a salad is the employment of borage blossoms and the tender upper leaves, in company or not with those of nasturtium, as a garnish or an ornament to salads, and still more as an addition to various cooling drinks. The best known of these beverages is cool tankard, composed of wine, water, lemon juice, sugar and borage flowers. To this "they seem to give additional coolness." They are often used similarly in lemonade, negus, claret-cup and fruit juice drinks.

The plant has possibly a still more important though undeveloped use as a bee forage. It is so easily grown and flowers so freely that it should be popular with apiarists, especially those who own or live near waste land, dry and stony tracts which they could sow to it. For such places it has an advantage over the many weeds which generally dispute possession in that it may be readily controlled by simple cultivation. It generally can hold its own against the plant populace of such places.

Caraway (*Carum carui*, Linn.), a biennial or an annual herb of the natural order Umbelliferæ. Its names, both popular and botanical, are supposed to be derived from Caria, in Asia Minor, where the plant is believed first to have attracted attention. From very early ages the caraway has been esteemed by cooks and doctors, between which a friendly rivalry might seem to exist, each vying to give it prominence. At the present time the cooks seem to be in the ascendancy; the seeds or their oil are rarely used in modern medicine, except to disguise the flavor of repulsive drugs.

Caraway for Comfits and Birthday Cakes

Since caraway seeds were found by O'Heer in the debris of the lake habitations of Switzerland, the fact seems well established that the plant is a native of Europe and the probability is increased that the *Careum* of Pliny is this same plant, as its use by Apicus would also indicate. It is mentioned in the twelfth-century writings as grown in Morocco, and in the thirteenth by the Arabs. As a spice, its use in England seems to have begun at the close of the fourteenth century. From its Asiatic home it spread first with Phoenician commerce to western Europe, whence by later voyageurs it has been carried throughout the civilized world. So widely has it been distributed that the traveler may find it in the wilds of Iceland and Scandinavia, the slopes of sunny Spain, the steeps of the Himalayas, the veldt of southern Africa, the bush of Australia, the prairies and the pampas of America.

Caraway is largely cultivated in Morocco, and is an important article of export from Russia, Prussia, and Holland. It has developed no clearly marked varieties; some specimens, however, seem to be more distinctly annual than others, though attempts to isolate these and thus secure a quick-maturing variety seem not to have been made.

Description.—The fleshy root, about ½ inch in diameter, is yellowish externally, whitish within, and has a slight carroty taste. From it a rosette of finely pinnated leaves is developed, and later the sparsely leaved, channeled, hollow, branching flower stem which rises from 18 to 30 inches and during early summer bears umbels of little white flowers followed by oblong, pointed, somewhat curved, light brown aromatic fruits—the caraway "seeds" of commerce. These retain their germinating power for about three years, require about 10,000 seeds to make an ounce and fifteen ounces to the quart.

Cultivation.—Frequently, if not usually, caraway is sown together with coriander in the same drills on heavy lands during May or early June. The coriander, being a quick-maturing plant, may be harvested before the caraway throws up a flowering stem. Thus two crops may be secured from the same land in the same time occupied by the caraway alone. Ordinary thinning to 6 or 8 inches between plants is done when the seedlings are established. Other requirements of the crop are all embraced in the practices of clean cultivation.

Harvest occurs in July of the year following the seeding. The plants are cut about 12 inches above ground with sickles, spread on sheets to dry for a few days, and later beaten with a light flail. After threshing, the seed must be spread thinly and turned daily until the last vestige of moisture has evaporated. From 400 to 800 pounds is the usual range of yield.

If seed be sown as soon as ripe, plants may be secured which mature earlier than the main crop. Thus six or eight weeks may be saved in the growing season, and by continuing such selection a quick-maturing strain may be secured with little effort. This would also obviate the trouble of keeping seed from one year to the next, for the strain would be practically a winter annual.

Uses.—Occasionally the leaves and young shoots are eaten either cooked or as an ingredient in salads. The roots, too, have been esteemed in some countries, even more highly than the parsnip, which, however, largely because of its size, has supplanted it for this purpose. But the seeds are the important part. They find popular use in bread, cheese, liquors, salads, sauces, soups, candy, and especially in seed cakes, cookies and comfits. The colorless or pale yellow essential oil distilled with water from the seeds, which contain between 5% and 7½% of it, has the characteristic flavor and odor of the fruit. It is extensively employed in the manufacture of toilet articles, such as perfumery, and especially soaps.

Catnip, or **cat mint** (*Nepeta cataria*, Linn.), a perennial herb of the natural order Labiatæ. The popular name is in allusion to the attraction the plant has for cats. They not only eat it, but rub themselves upon it purring with delight. The generic name is derived from the Etrurian city Neptic, in the neighborhood of which various species of the genus formerly became prominent.

Like several of its relatives catnip is a well-known weed. It has become naturalized in America, and is most frequently observed in dry, waste places, especially in the East, though it is also often found in gardens and around dwellings throughout the United States and Canada.

Description.—Its erect, square, branching stems, from 18 to 36 inches tall, bear notched oval or heartshaped leaves, whitish below, and during late summer terminal clusters of white flowers in small heads, far apart below, but crowded close above. The fruits are small, brown, ovoid, smooth and with three clearly defined angles. An ounce contains about 3,400 seeds. Viability lasts for five years.

Catnip, Pussy's Delight

Cultivation. Catnip will grow with the most ordinary attention on any fairly dry soil. The seed need only be sown in autumn or spring where the plants are to remain or in a nursery bed for subsequent transplanting. If to be kept in a garden bed they should stand 18 to 24 inches apart each way. Nothing is needful except to keep down weeds in order to have them succeed for several years on the same spot.

Uses.—The most important use of the plant is as a bee forage; for this purpose waste places are often planted to catnip. As a condiment the leaves were formerly in popular use, especially in the form of sauces; but milder flavors are now more highly esteemed. Still, the French use catnip to a considerable extent. Like many of its relatives, catnip was a popular medicinal remedy for many fleshly ills; now it is practically relegated to domestic medicine. Even in this it is a moribund remedy for infant flatulence, and is clung to only by unlettered nurses of a passing generation.

Chervil (*Scandix Cerefolium,* Linn.), a southern Europe annual, with stems about 18 inches tall and bearing few divided leaves composed of oval, much-cut leaflets. The small white flowers, borne in umbels, are followed by long, pointed, black seeds with a conspicuous furrow from end to end. These seeds, which retain their germinability about three years, but are rather difficult to keep, may be sown where the plants are to stay, at any season, about eight weeks before a crop is desired; cultivation is like that of parsley. During summer and in warm climates, cool, shady situations should be chosen, otherwise any situation and soil are suitable. The leaves, which are highly aromatic, are used, especially in France and England, for seasoning and for mixed salads. Chervil is rarely used alone, but is the chief ingredient in what the French call *fines herbes*, a mixture which finds its way into a host of culinary concoctions. The best variety is the Curled, which, though it has the same flavor as the plain, is a prettier garnish.

Chives (*Allium Schœnoprasum*, Linn.), a bulbous, onion-like perennial belonging to the Liliaceæ. Naturally the plants form thick tufts of abundant, hollow, grasslike leaves from their little oval bulbs and mat of fibrous roots. The short flower stems bear terminal clusters of generally sterile flowers. Hence the plants are propagated by planting the individual bulbs or by division of clumps in early spring. Frequently chives are planted in flower borders as an edging, for which purpose the compact growth and dainty flowers particularly recommend them. They should not be allowed to grow in the same place more than three years.

Strictly speaking, chives do not belong with the herbs, but their leaves are so frequently used instead of onions for flavoring salads, stews and other dishes, and reference has been so often made to them in these pages, that a brief description has been included. For market the clumps are cut in squares and the whole plant sold. Treated in this way the greengrocers can keep them in good condition by watering until sold. For use the leaves are cut with shears close to the ground. If allowed to stand in the garden, cuttings may be made at intervals of two or three weeks all through the season.

Clary (*Salvia sclarea*, Linn.), a perennial herb of the natural order

Labiatæ. The popular name is a corruption of the specific. In the discussion on sage will be found the significance of the generic name. Syria is said to be the original home of clary, but Italy is also mentioned. The presumption is in favor of the former country, as it is the older, and the plant was probably carried westward from it by soldiers or merchants. In England clary was known prior to 1538, when Turner published his garden lore, but in America, except in foreigners' gardens, it is rarely seen. It has been listed in seedsmen's catalogs since 1806.

Description.—The large, very broad, oblong, obtuse, toothed, woolly haired, radical leaves are grayish green and somewhat rumpled like those of Savoy cabbage. From among them rise the 2-foot tall, square, branching, sparsely leaved stems, which during the second year bear small clusters of lilac or white showy flowers in long spikes. The smooth brown or marbled shining seeds retain their germinating power for three years.

Cultivation.—The plants thrive in any well-drained soil. Seed may be sown during March in drills 18 inches apart where the plants are to remain or in a seedbed for transplanting 18 inches asunder in May. Clean cultivation is needed throughout the summer until the plants have full possession of the ground. In August the leaves may be gathered, and if this harvest be judiciously done the production of foliage should continue until midsummer of the second year, when the plants will probably insist upon flowering. After this it is best to rely upon new plants for supplies of leaves, the old plants being pulled.

Uses.—In America, the leaves are little used in cookery, and even in Europe they seem to be less popular than formerly, sage having taken their place. Wine is sometimes made from the plant when in flower. As an ornamental, clary is worth a place in the hardy flower border.

Coriander (*Coriandrum sativum*, Linn.), "a plant of little beauty and of easiest culture," is a hardy annual herb of the natural order Umbelliferæ. The popular name is derived from the generic, which comes from the ancient Greek Koris, a kind of bug, in allusion to the disagreeable odor of the foliage and other green parts. The specific name refers to its cultivation in gardens. Hence the scientific name declares it to be the cultivated buggy-smelling plant.

**Coriander, for
Old-Fashioned Candies**

Coriander has been cultivated from such ancient times that its land of nativity is unknown, though it is said to be a native of southern Europe and of China. It has been used in cookery and of course, too, in medicine; for, according to ancient reasoning, anything with so pronounced and unpleasant an odor must necessarily possess powerful curative or preventive attributes! Its seeds have been found in Egyptian tombs of the 21st dynasty. Many centuries later Pliny wrote that the best quality of seed still came to Italy from Egypt. Prior to the Norman conquest in 1066, the plant was well known in Great Britain, probably having been taken there by the early Roman conquerors. Before 1670 it was introduced into Massachusetts. During this long period of cultivation there seems to be no record or even indication of varieties. In many temperate and tropical countries it has become a frequent weed in cultivated fields.

Description.—From a cluster of slightly divided radical leaves branching stems rise to heights of 2 to 2½ feet. Toward their summits they bear much divided leaves, with linear segments and umbels of small whitish flowers, followed by pairs of united, hemispherical, brownish-yellow, deeply furrowed "seeds," about the size of a sweet pea seed. These retain their vitality for five or six years. The seeds do not have the unpleasant odor of the plant, but have a rather agreeable smell and a moderately warm, pungent taste.

Cultivation.—Coriander, a plant of the easiest culture, does best in a rather light, warm, friable soil. In Europe it is often sown with caraway, which, being a biennial and producing only a rosette of leaves at the surface of the ground the first year, is not injured when the annual coriander is cut. The seed is often sown in the autumn, though spring sowing is perhaps in more favor. The rows are made about 15 inches apart, the seeds dropped 1 inch asunder and ½ inch deep and the plantlets thinned to 6 or 8 inches. Since the plants run to seed quickly, they must be watched and cut early to prevent loss and consequent seeding of the ground. After curing in the shade the seed is threshed as already described (see **page 24**). On favorable land the yield may reach or even exceed 1,500 pounds to the acre.

Uses.—Some writers say the young leaves of the plant are used in salads and for seasoning soups, dressings, etc. If this is so, I can only remark that there is no accounting for tastes. I am inclined to think, however, that these writers are drawing upon their imagination or have been "stuffed" by people who take pleasure in supplying misinformation. The odor is such as to suggest the flavor of "buggy" raspberries we sometimes gather in the fence rows. Any person who relishes buggy berries may perhaps enjoy coriander salad or soup.

Only the seed is of commercial importance. It is used largely in making comfits and other kinds of confectionery, for adding to bread, and, especially in the East, as an ingredient in curry powder and other condiments. In medicine its chief use now is to disguise the taste of disagreeable drugs. Distillers use it for flavoring various kinds of liquors.

Cumin (*Cuminum Cyminum*, Linn.), a low-growing annual herb of the Nile valley, but cultivated in the Mediterranean region, Arabia, Egypt, Morocco, India, China, and Palestine from very early times, (See Isaiah xviii, 25-27 and Matthew xxiii, 23.) Pliny is said to have considered it the best appetizer of all condiments. During the middle ages it was in very common use. All the old herbals of the sixteenth and the seventeenth centuries figure and describe and extol it. In Europe it is extensively cultivated in Malta and Sicily, and will mature seed as far north as Norway; in America, today, the seed is cataloged by some seedsmen, but very little is grown.

Description.—The plant is very diminutive, rarely exceeding a height of 6 inches. Its stems, which branch freely from the base, bear mere linear leaves and small lilac flowers, in little umbels of 10 to 20 blossoms each. The six-ribbed, elongated "seeds" in appearance resemble caraway seeds, but are straighter, lighter and larger, and in formation are like the double seeds of coriander, convex on one side and concave on the other. They bear long hairs, which fold up when the seed is dry.

After the seed has been kept for two years it begins to lose its germinating power, but will sprout reasonably well when three years old. It is characterized by a peculiar, strong aromatic odor, and a hot taste.

Culture.—As soon as the ground has become warm the seed is sown in drills about 15 inches apart where the plants are to remain. Except for keeping down the weeds no further attention is necessary. The plants mature in about two months, when the stems are cut and dried in the shade. (See **page 24**.) The seeds are used in India as an ingredient in curry powder, in France for flavoring pickles, pastry and soups.

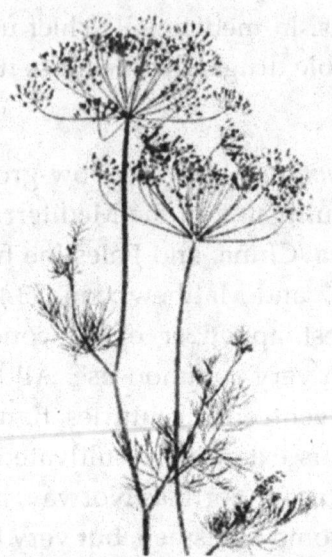

Dill, of Pickle Fame

Dill (*Anethum graveolens*, Linn.), a hardy annual, native of the Mediterranean and the Black Sea regions, smaller than common fennel, which it somewhat resembles both in appearance and in the flavor of the green parts, which are, however, less agreeable.

In ancient times it was grown in Palestine. The word translated, "anise" in Matthew xxiii, 23, is said to have been "dill" in the original Greek. It was well known in Pliny's time, and is often discussed by writers in the middle ages. According to American writings, it has been grown in this country for more than 100 years and has become spontaneous in many places.

Description.—Ordinarily the plants grow 2 to 2½ feet tall. The glaucous, smooth, hollow, branching stems bear very threadlike leaves and in midsummer compound umbels with numerous yellow flowers, whose small petals are rolled inward. Very flat, pungent, bitter seeds are freely produced, and unless gathered early are sure to stock the garden with volunteer seedlings for the following year. Under fair storage conditions, the seeds continue viable for three years. They are rather light; a quart of them weighs about 11 ounces, and an ounce is said to contain over 25,000 seeds.

Cultivation.—Where dill has not already been grown seed may be sown in early spring, preferably in a warm sandy soil, where the plants are to remain. Any well-drained soil will do. The drills should be 1 foot apart, the seeds scattered thinly and covered very shallow; a bed 12 feet square should supply abundance of seed for any ordinary family. To sow this area ¼ to ½ ounce of seed is ample. For field use the rows may be 15 inches apart and the seed sown more thinly. It should not be covered much more than ¼ inch. Some growers favor fall sowing, because they claim the seed is more likely to germinate than in the spring, and also to produce better plants than spring-sown seed.

At all times the plants must be kept free from weeds and the soil loose and open. When three or four weeks old the seedlings are thinned to 9 inches, or even a foot apart. As soon as the seed is ripe, shortly after midsummer, it must be gathered with the least possible shaking and handling, so as to prevent loss. It is well to place the stems as cut directly in a tight-bottomed cart or a wheelbarrow, with a canvas receptacle for the purpose, and to haul direct to the shade where drying is to occur. A good place for this is a barn, upon the floor of which a large canvas sheet is spread, and where a free circulation of air can be secured. (See **page 24**.)

Uses.—The French use dill for flavoring preserves, cakes and pastry. For these purposes it is of too strong and pronounced a character to be relished by American palates. The seeds perhaps more often appear in soups, sauces and stews, but even here they are relished more by our European residents than by native Americans. Probably they are most used in pickles, especially in preserving cucumbers according to German recipes. Thousands of barrels of such pickles are sold annually, more especially in the larger cities and to the poorer people; but as this pickle is procurable at all delicatessen stores, it has gained great popularity among even the well-to-do. An oil is distilled from the seeds and used in perfuming soap. The young leaves are said to be used in pickles, soups and sauces, and even in salads. For the last purpose they are rather strong to suit most people, and for the others the seeds are far more popular.

Dill vinegar is a popular household condiment. It is made by soaking the seed in good vinegar for a few days before using. The quantity of ingredients to use is immaterial. Only a certain amount of the flavor can be dissolved by the vinegar, and as few samples of vinegar are alike, the quantities both to mix and of the decoction to use must be left to the housewife. This may be said, however, that after one lot of seed has been treated the vinegar may be poured off and the seeds steeped a second time to get a weaker infusion. The two infusions may then be mixed and kept in a dark cupboard for use as needed.

Fennel (*Fœniculum officinale*, All.), a biennial or perennial herb, generally considered a native of southern Europe, though common on all Mediterranean shores. The old Latin name *Fœniculum* is derived from *fœnum* or hay. It has spread with civilization, especially where Italians have colonized, and may be found growing wild in many parts of the world, upon dry soils near the sea coast and upon river banks.

Sweet Fennel

It seems to be partial to limestone soils, such as the chalky lands of England and the shelly formation of Bermuda. In this latter community I have seen it thriving upon cliffs where there seemed to be only a pinch of soil, and where the rock was so dry and porous that it would crumble to coarse dust when crushed in the hand. The plant was cultivated by the ancient Romans for its aromatic fruits and succulent, edible shoots. Whether cultivated in northern Europe at that time is not certain, but it is frequently mentioned in Anglo-Saxon cookery prior to the Norman conquest. Charlemagne ordered its culture upon the imperial farms. At present it is most popular in Italy, and France. In America it is in most demand among French and Italians. Like many other plants, fennel has had a highly interesting career from a medical point of view. But it no longer plays even a "small part" in the drama. Hints as to its history may be found on **page 50**.

Description.—Common garden or long, sweet fennel is distinguished from its wild or better relative (*F. vulgare*) by having much stouter, taller (5 to 6 feet) tubular and larger stems, less divided, more glaucous leaves. But a still more striking difference is seen in the leaf stalks which form a curved sheath around the stem even as far up as the base of the leaf above. Then, too, the green flowers are borne on more sturdy pedicels in the broader umbels, lastly the seeds are double the size of the wild fennel seeds, ¼ or ½ inch long. They are convex on one side, flat on the other, and are marked by five yellowish ribs. Though a French writer says the seed degenerates "promptly," and recommends the use of fresh seed annually, it will not be wise to throw away any where it is not wanted to germinate, unless it is over four years old, as seed as old even as that is said to be satisfactory for planting.

Cultivation.—In usual garden practice fennel is propagated by seeds, and is grown as an annual instead of as a biennial or a perennial. The plants will flourish in almost any well-drained soil, but seem to prefer light loams of a limy nature. It is not particular as to exposure. The seed may be sown in nursery beds or where the plants are to remain. In the beds, the drills may be 6 inches apart, and not more than 1-3 inch deep, or the seed may be scattered broadcast. An ounce will be enough for a bed 10 feet square. When the plants are about 3 inches tall they should be transplanted 15 or 18 inches asunder in rows 2 to 2½ feet apart. Some growers sow in late summer and in autumn so as to have early crops the following season; they also make several successional sowings at intervals of one or two weeks, in order to supply the demands of their customers for fresh fennel stalks from midsummer to December or even later. The plants will grow more or less in very cold, that is, not actually freezing weather.

If sown in place, the rows should be the suggested 2 to 2½ feet apart, and the plants thinned several times until the required distance is reached. Thinnings may be used for culinary purposes. For family use half an ounce of seed, if fairly fresh, will produce an ample supply of plants, and for several years, either from the established roots or by reseeding. Unless seed is needed for household or sowing purposes, the flower stems should be cut as soon as they appear.

Uses.—Fennel is considered indispensable in French and Italian cookery. The young plants and the tender leaves are often used for garnishes and to add flavor to salads. They are also minced and added to sauces usually served with puddings. The tender stems and the leaves are employed in soups and fish sauces, though more frequently they are eaten raw as a salad with or without dressing. The famous "Carosella" of Naples consists of the stems cut when the plant is about to bloom. These stems are considered a great delicacy served raw with the leaf stalks still around them. Oil, vinegar and pepper are eaten with them. By sowing at intervals of a week or 10 days Italian gardeners manage to have a supply almost all the year.

The seeds are used in cookery, confectionery and for flavoring liquors. Oil of fennel, a pale yellow liquid, with a sweetish aromatic odor and flavor, is distilled with water. It is used in perfumery and for scenting soaps. A pound of oil is the usual yield of 500 pounds of the plant.

Finocchio, or **Florence fennel** (*F. dulce*, D. C.), deserves special mention here. It appears to be a native of Italy, a distinct dwarf annual, very thick-set herb. The stem joints are so close together and their bases so swelled as to suggest malformation. Even when full grown and producing seed, the plant rarely exceeds 2 feet. The large, finely cut, light green leaves are borne on very broad, pale green or almost whitish stalks, which overlap at their bases, somewhat like celery, but much more swelled at edible maturity, to form a sort of head or irregular ball, the "apple," as it is called, sometimes as large as a man's fist. The seeds are a peculiar oblong, much broader than long, convex on one side and flat on the other, with five conspicuous ribs.

Cultivation is much the same as for common fennel, though owing to the dwarf nature of the plant the rows and the plants may be closer together. The seedlings should be 5 or 6 inches asunder. They are very thirsty things and require water frequently. When the "apple" attains the size of an egg, earth may be drawn up slightly to the base, which may be about half covered; cutting may begin about 10 days later. Florence fennel is generally boiled and served with either a butter or a cream dressing. It suggests celery in flavor, but is sweeter and is even more pleasingly fragrant. In Italy it is one of the commonest and most popular of vegetables. In other European countries it is also well known, but in America its cultivation is almost confined to Italian gardens or to such as supply Italian demands in the large cities. In New York it is commonly sold by greengrocers and pushcart men in the Italian sections.

Fennel Flower (*Nigella sativa*, Linn.), an Asiatic annual, belonging to the Ranunculaceæ, grown to a limited extent in southern Europe, but scarcely known in America. Among the Romans it was esteemed in cookery, hence one of its common names, Roman coriander. The plant has a rather stiff, erect, branching stem, bears deeply cut grayish-green leaves and terminal grayish-blue flowers, which precede odd, toothed, seed vessels filled with small, triangular, black, highly aromatic seeds. For garden use the seed is sown in spring after the ground gets warm. The drills may be 15 to

18 inches apart and the plants thinned to 10 or 12 inches asunder. No special attention is necessary until midsummer, when the seed ripens. These are easily threshed and cleaned. After drying they should be stored in sacks in a cool, dry place. They are used just as they are or like dill in cookery.

Hoarhound, or **horehound** (*Marrubium vulgare*, Linn.), a perennial plant of the natural order Labiatæ, formerly widely esteemed in cookery and medicine, but now almost out of use except for making candy which some people still eat in the belief that it relieves tickling in the throat due to coughing. In many parts of the world hoarhound has become naturalized on dry, poor soils, and is even a troublesome weed in such situations. Bees are very partial to hoarhound nectar, and make a pleasing honey from the flowers where these are abundant. This honey has been almost as popular as hoarhound candy, and formerly was obtainable at druggists. Except in isolated sections, it has ceased to be sold in the drug stores. The generic name *Marrubium* is derived from a Hebrew word meaning bitter. The flavor is so strong and lasting that the modern palate wonders how the ancient mouth could stand such a thing in cookery.

The numerous branching, erect stems and the almost square, toothed, grayish-green leaves are covered with a down from which the common name hoarhound is derived. The white flowers, borne in axillary clusters forming whorls and spikes, are followed by small, brown, oblong seeds pointed at one end. These may be sown up to the third year after ripening with the expectation that they will grow. Spring is the usual time for sowing. A dry, poor soil, preferably exposed to the south, should be chosen. The plants may stand 12 to 15 inches apart. After once becoming established no further attention need be given except to prevent seed forming, thus giving the plant less chance to become a nuisance. Often the clumps may be divided or layers or cuttings may be used for propagation. No protection need be given, as the plants are hardy.

An old author gives the following recipe for hoarhound candy: To one pint of a strong decoction of the leaves and stems or the roots add 8 or 10 pounds of sugar. Boil to candy height and pour into molds or small paper cases previously well dusted with finely powdered lump sugar, or pour on dusted marble slabs and cut in squares.

Hyssop (*Hyssopus officinalis*, Linn.), a perennial evergreen undershrub of the Labiatæ, native of the Mediterranean region. Though well known in ancient times, this plant is probably not the one known as hyssop in Biblical writings. According to the Standard Dictionary the Biblical "hyssop" is "an unidentified plant ... thought by some to have been a species of marjoram (*Origanum maru*); by others, the caper-bush (*Capparis spinosa*); and by the author of the 'History of Bible Plants,' to have been the name of any common article in the form of a brush or a broom." In ancient and medieval times hyssop was grown for its fancied medicinal qualities, for ornament and for cookery. Except for ornament, it is now very little cultivated. Occasionally it is found growing wild in other than Mediterranean countries.

Description.—The smooth, simple stems, which grow about 2 feet tall, bear lanceolate-linear, entire leaves and small clusters of usually blue, though sometimes pink or white flowers, crowded in terminal spikes. The small, brown, glistening three-angled seeds, which have a little white hilum near their apices, retain their viability three years. Leaves, stems and flowers possess a highly aromatic odor and a hot, bitter flavor.

Cultivation.—Hyssop succeeds best in rather warm, limy soil. It may be readily propagated by division, cuttings, and seed. In cold climates the last way is the most common. Seed is sown in early spring, either in a cold frame or in the open ground, and the seedlings transplanted in early summer. Even where the plants survive the winters, it is advisable to renew them every three or four years. When grown in too rich soil, the growth will be very lush and will lack aroma. Plants should stand not closer than 6 inches in the rows, which should be at least 18 inches apart. They do best in partial shade.

Uses.—Hyssop has almost entirely disappeared from culinary practice because it is too strong-flavored. Its tender leaves and shoots are, however, occasionally added to salads, to supply a bitter taste. The colorless oil distilled from the leaves has a peculiar odor and an acrid, camphorescent taste. Upon contact with the air it turns yellow and changes to a resin. From 400 to 500 pounds of the fresh plant yield a pound of oil. The oil is used to some extent in the preparation of toilet articles.

Lavender, (*Lavendula vera*, D. C.; *L. Angustifolia*, Moench.; *L. spica*, Linn.), a half-hardy perennial undershrub, native of dry, calcareous uplands in southern Europe. Its name is derived from the Latin word *Lavo*, to wash, a distillation of the flowers being anciently used in perfuming water for washing the body. The plant forms a compact clump 2 to 2½ feet tall, has numerous erect stems, bearing small, linear gray leaves, above which the slender, square, flower stems arise. The small violet-blue flowers are arranged in a short, terminal spike, and are followed by little brown, oblong, shiny seeds, with white dots at the ends, attached to the plant. The seeds remain viable for about five years.

Cultivation.—Lavender succeeds best on light, limy or chalky soil, but will do well in any good loam. In gardens it is usually employed as an edging for flower beds, and is most frequently propagated by division or cuttings, seed being used only to get a start where plants cannot be secured in the other ways mentioned. In cold climates the plants must either be protected or removed to a greenhouse, or at least a cold frame, which can be covered in severe weather. The seed is sown indoors during March, and if crowding, pricked out 2 inches asunder. When the ground has become warm, the plants are set in the open 15 to 20 inches asunder. It delights in a sunny situation, and is most fragrant on poor soil. Rich soil makes the plant larger but the flowers poorer in perfume.

Uses.—The plant is sometimes grown for a condiment and an addition to salads, dressings, etc., but its chief use is in perfumery, the flowers being gathered and either dried for use in sachet bags or distilled for their content of oil. In former years no girl was supposed to be ready for marriage until, with her own hands, she had made her own linen and stored it with lavender. And in some sections the lavender is still used, though the linen is nowadays purchased.

In southern France and in England considerable areas are devoted to lavender for the perfumery business. The flower stems are cut in August, covered at once with bast matting to protect them from the sun and taken to the stills to obtain the thin, pale yellow, fragrant oil. Four-year-old plants yield the greatest amount of oil, but the product is greater from a two-year plantation than from an older one, the plants then being most vigorous. Two grades of oil are made, the best being used for lavender water, the poorer for soap making. In a good season about one pound of oil is obtained from 150 to 200 pounds of the cut plants.

Lovage (*Levisticum officinale*, Koch.), a perennial, native of the Mediterranean region. The large, dark-green, shining radical leaves are usually divided into two or three segments. Toward the top the thick, hollow, erect stems divide to form opposite, whorled branches which bear umbels of yellow flowers, followed by highly aromatic, hollowed fruits ("seeds") with three prominent ribs. Propagation is by division or by seeds not over three years old. In late summer when the seed ripens, it is sown and the seedlings transplanted either in the fall or as early in spring as possible to their permanent places. Rich, moist soil is needed. Root division is performed in early spring. With cultivation and alternation like that given to Angelica, the plants should last for several years.

Formerly lovage was used for a great variety of purposes, but nowadays it is restricted almost wholly to confectionery, the young stems being handled like those of Angelica. So far as I have been able to learn, the leaf stalks and stem bases, which were formerly blanched like celery, are no longer used in this way.

Marigold (*Calendula officinalis*, Linn.), an annual herb of the natural order Compositæ, native of southern Europe. Its Latin name, suggestive of its flowering habit, signifies blooming through the months. Our word calendar is of the same derivation. Its short stems, about 12 inches tall, branch near their bases, bear lanceolate, oblong, unpleasantly scented leaves, and showy yellow or orange flowers in heads. The curved, gray seeds, which are rough, wrinkled and somewhat spiny, retain their germinating power for about three years.

Cultivation.—For the garden the seed is usually started in a hotbed during March or April and the plants pricked out in flats 2 inches apart and hardened off in the usual way. When the weather becomes settled they are set a foot or 15 inches apart in rather poor soil, preferably light and sandy, with sunny exposure. Often the seed is sown in the open and the seedlings thinned and transplanted when about 2 inches tall.

Uses.—The flower heads are sometimes dried and used in broths, soups, stews, etc., but the flavor is too pronounced for American palates. One gardener remarked that "only a few plants are needed by a family." I think that two would produce about twice as much as I would care to use in a century. For culinary use the flowers are gathered when in full bloom, dried in the shade and stored in glass jars. The fresh flowers have often been used to color butter.

The marigold, "homely forgotten flower, under the rose's bower, plain as a weed," to quote Bayard Taylor, is a general favorite flowering plant, especially in country gardens. It is so easily grown, is so free a bloomer, and under ordinary management continues from early summer until even hard frosts arrive, that busy farmers wives and daughters love it. Then, too, it is one of the old-fashioned flowers, about which so many happy thoughts cling. What more beautiful and suggestive lines could one wish than these:

> "The marigold, whose courtier's face
> Echoes the sun, and doth unlace
> Her at his rise, at his full stop

Packs up and shuts her gaudy shop."

—*John Cleveland*
"On Phillis Walking before Sunrise"

"Youth! Youth! how buoyant are thy hopes! They turn
Like marigolds toward the sunny side,"

—*Jean Ingelow*
"The Four Bridges"

Sweet Marjoram

Marjoram.—Two species of marjoram now grown for culinary purposes (several others were formerly popular) are members of the Labiatæ or mint family—pot or perennial marjoram (*Origanum vulgare*, Linn.) and sweet or annual (*O. Marjorana*). Really, both plants are perennials, but sweet marjoram, because of its liability to be killed by frost, is so commonly cultivated in cold countries as an annual that it has acquired this name, which readily distinguishes it from its hardy relative. Perennial marjoram is a native of Europe, but has become naturalized in many cool and even cold temperate climates. It is often found wild in the Atlantic states in the borders of woods.

The general name *origanum*, meaning delight of the mountain, is derived from two Greek words, *oros*, mountain; and *ganos*, joy, some of the species being found commonly upon mountain sides. Under cultivation it has developed a few varieties the most popular of which are a variegated form used for ornamental purposes, and a dwarf variety noted for its ability to come true to seed. Both varieties are used in cookery. The perennial species seems to have had the longer association with civilization; at least it is the one identified in the writings of Pliny, Albertus Magnus and the English herbalists of the middle ages. Annual marjoram is thought to be the species considered sacred in India to Vishnu and Siva.

Description.—Perennial marjoram rises even 2 feet high, in branchy clumps, bears numerous short-stemmed, ovate leaves about 1 inch long, and terminal clusters or short spikes of little, pale lilac or pink blossoms and purple bracts. The oval, brown seeds are very minute. They are, however, heavy for their size, since a quart of them weighs about 24 ounces. I am told that an ounce contains more than 340,000, and would rather believe than be forced to prove it.

Annual marjoram is much more erect, more bush-like, has smaller, narrower leaves, whiter flowers, green bracts and larger, but lighter seeds—only 113,000 to the ounce and only 20 ounces to the quart!

Cultivation.—Perennial marjoram when once established may be readily propagated by cuttings, division or layers, but it is so easy to grow from seed that this method is usually employed. There is little danger of its becoming a weed, because the seedlings are easily destroyed while small. The seed should be sown during March or April in flats or beds that can be protected from rain. It is merely dusted on the surface, the soil being pressed down slightly with a board or a brick. Until the seedlings appear, the bed should be shaded to check evaporation. When the plants are 2 or 3 inches tall they may be transplanted to the places where they are to remain, as they are not so easy to transplant as lettuce and geraniums. The work should be done while the plants are very small, and larger numbers should be set than will ultimately be allowed to grow. I have had no difficulty in transplanting, but some people who have had prefer to sow the seed where the plants are to stand.

If to be used for edging, the dwarf plants may be set 3 or 6 inches apart; the larger kinds require a foot or 15 inches in which to develop. In field cultivation the greater distance is the more desirable. From the very start the plants must be kept free from weeds and the soil loose and open. Handwork is essential until they become established. The plants will last for years.

Annual marjoram is managed in the same kind of way as to seeding and cultivation; but as the plant is tender, fresh sowings must be made annually. To be sure, plants may be taken up in the fall and used for making cuttings or layers towards spring for the following seasons beds. As annual marjoram is somewhat smaller than the perennial kind (except the dwarf perennial variety), the distances may be somewhat less, say 9 or 10 inches. Annual marjoram is a quick-growing plant—so quick, in fact, that leaves may be secured within six or eight weeks of sowing. The flowers appear in 10 to 12 weeks, and the seed ripens soon after.

When it is desired to cure the leaves for winter use, the stems should be cut just as the flowers begin to appear, and dried in the usual manner. (See **page 22**.) If seed is wanted, they should be cut soon after the flowers fall or even before all have fallen—when the scales around the seeds begin to look as if drying. The cut stems must be dried on sheets of very fine weave, to prevent loss of seed. When the leaves are thoroughly dry they must be thrashed and rubbed before being placed in sieves, first of coarse, and then of finer mesh.

Uses.—The leaves and the flower and tender stem tips of both species have a pleasant odor, and are used for seasoning soups, stews, dressings and sauces. They are specially favored in France and Italy, but are popular also in England and America. In France marjoram is cultivated commercially for its oil, a thin, light yellow or greenish liquid, with the concentrated odor of marjoram and peppermint. It has a warm, and slightly bitter taste. About 200 pounds of stems and leaves are needed to get a pound of oil. Some distillation is done in England, where 70 pounds of the plant yield about one ounce of oil. This oil is used for perfuming toilet articles, especially soap, but is perhaps less popular than the essential oil of thyme.

Mint (*Mentha viridis*, Linn.)—Spearmint, a member of the Labiatæ, is a very hardy perennial, native to Mediterranean countries. Its generic name is derived from the mythological origin ascribed to it. Poets declared that Proserpine became jealous of Cocytus's daughter, Minthe, whom she transformed into the plant. The specific name means green, hence the common name, green mint, often applied to it. The old Jewish law did not require that tithes of "mint, anise and cumin" should be paid in to the treasury, but the Pharisees paid them while omitting the weightier matters, justice, mercy, and faith (Matthew xxiii, 23). From this and many other references in old writings it is evident that mint has been highly esteemed for many centuries. In the seventeenth century John Gerarde wrote concerning it that "the smelle rejoyceth the heart of man." Indeed, it has been so universally esteemed that it is found wild in nearly all countries to which civilization has extended. It has been known as an escape from American gardens for about 200 years, and is sometimes troublesome as a weed in moist soil.

Mint, Best Friend of Roast Lamb

Description.—From creeping rootstocks erect square stems rise to a height of about 2 feet, and near their summits bear spreading branches with very short-stemmed, acute-pointed, lance-shaped, wrinkled leaves with toothed edges, and cylindrical spikes of small pink or lilac flowers, followed by very few, roundish, minute, brown seeds.

Cultivation.—The plant may be easily propagated by means of cuttings, offsets and division in spring. They may be expected to yield somewhat of a crop the first season, but much more the second. In field culture they will continue profitable for several years, provided that each autumn the tops are cut off near the ground and a liberal dressing of manure, compost or even rich soil is given. In ordinary garden practice it is well also to observe this plan, but usually mint is there allowed to shift for itself, along with the horseradish and the Jerusalem artichoke when such plants are grown. So treated, it is likely to give trouble, because, having utilized the food in one spot, its stems seek to migrate to better quarters. Hence, if the idea is to neglect the plants, a corner of the garden should be chosen where there is no danger of their becoming a nuisance. It is best to avoid all such trouble by renewing or changing the beds every 5 or 6 years.

Mint will grow anywhere but does best in a moist, rich loam and partial shade. If in a sheltered spot, it will start earlier in the spring than if exposed. Upon an extensive scale the drills should be 2 inches deep and 12 to 15 inches apart. Bits of the rootstocks are dropped at intervals of 6 to 12 inches in the rows and covered with a wheel hoe. For a new plantation the rootstocks should be secured when the stems have grown 2 or 3 inches tall.

For forcing, the clumps are lifted in solid masses, with the soil attached, and placed in hotbeds or forcing house benches. Three or four inches of moist soil is worked in among and over them and watered freely as soon as growth starts. Cuttings may be made in two or three weeks. Often mint is so grown in lettuce and violet houses both upon and under the benches. During winter and spring there is enough of a demand for the young tender stems and leaves to make the plants pay. It is said that the returns from an ordinary 3 x 6-foot hotbed sash should be $10 to $15 for the winter. For drying, the stems should be cut on a dry day when the plants are approaching full bloom and after the dew has disappeared in the morning. They should be spread out very thinly in the shade or in an airy shed. (See **page 22**.) If cut during damp weather, there is danger of the leaves turning black.

Uses.—In both the green and the dried state mint is widely used in Europe for flavoring soups, stews and sauces for meats of unpronounced character. Among the Germans pulverized mint is commonly upon the table in cruets for dusting upon gravies and soups, especially pea and bean purees.

In England and America the most universal use of mint is for making mint sauce, *the* sauce *par excellence* with roast spring lamb. Nothing can be simpler than to mince the tender tops and leaves very, very finely, add to vinegar and sweeten to taste. Many people fancy they don't like roast lamb. The chances are that they have never eaten it with wellmade mint sauce. In recent years mint jelly has been taking the place of the sauce, and perhaps justly, because it can not only be kept indefinitely without deterioration, but because it looks and is more tempting. It may be made by steeping mint leaves in apple jelly or in one of the various kinds of commercial gelatins so popular for making cold fruit puddings. The jelly should be a delicate shade of green. Of course, before pouring into the jelly glasses, the liquid is strained through a jelly bag to remove all particles of mint. A handful of leaves should color and flavor four to six glasses full.

Parsley (*Carum Petroselinum*, Linn.), a hardy biennial herb of the natural order Umbelliferæ, native to Mediterranean shores, and cultivated for at least 2,000 years. The specific name is derived from the habitat of the plant, which naturally grows among rocks, the Greek word for which is *petros*. Many of the ancient writings contain references to it, and some give directions for its cultivation.

The writings of the old herbalists of the 15th century show that in their times it had already developed several well-defined forms and numerous varieties, always a sure sign that a plant is popular. Throughout the world today it is unquestionably the most widely grown of all garden herbs, and has the largest number of varieties. In moist, moderately cool climates, it may be found wild as a weed, but nowhere has it become a pest.

"Ah! the green parsley, the thriving tufts of dill;
These again shall rise, shall live the coming year."

— *Moschus*

Curled Parsley

Description.—Like most biennials, parsley develops only a rosette of leaves during the first year. These leaves are dark green, long stalked and divided two or three times into ovate, wedge-shaped segments, and each division either entire, as in parsnip, or more or less finely cut or "curled." During the second season the erect, branched, channeled flower stems rise 2 feet or more high, and at their extremities bear umbels of little greenish flowers. The fruits or "seeds" are light brown or gray, convex on one side and flat on the other two, the convex side marked with fine ribs. They retain their germinating power for three years. An interesting fact, observed by Palladius in 210 A. D., is that old seed germinates more freely than freshly gathered seed.

Cultivation.—Parsley is so easily grown that no garden, and indeed no household, need be without it. After once passing the infant stage no difficulty need be experienced. It will thrive in any ordinary soil and will do well in a window box with only a moderate amount of light, and that not even direct sunshine. Gardeners often grow it beneath benches in greenhouses, where it gets only small amounts of light. No one need hesitate to plant it.

The seed is very slow in germinating, often requiring four to six weeks unless soaked before sowing. A full day's soaking in tepid water is none too long to wake up the germs. The drills may be made in a cold frame during March or in the open ground during April.

It is essential that parsley be sown very early in order to germinate at all. If sown late, it may possibly not get enough moisture to sprout, and if so it will fail completely. When sown in cold frames or beds for transplanting, the rows may be only 3 or 4 inches apart, though it is perhaps better, when such distances are chosen, to sow each alternate row to forcing radishes, which will have been marketed by the time the parsley seedlings appear. In the open ground the drills should be 12 to 15 inches apart, and the seed planted somewhat deeper and farther apart than in the presumably better-prepared seedbed or cold frame. One inch between seeds is none too little.

In field culture and at the distances mentioned six or seven pounds of seed will be needed for the acre. For cultivation on a smaller scale an ounce may be found sufficient for 50 to 100 feet of drill. This quantity should be enough for any ordinary-sized family. In all open ground culture the radish is the parsley's best friend, because it not only marks the rows, and thus helps early cultivation, but the radishes break, loosen and shade the soil and thus aid the parsley plants.

When the first thinning is done during May, the parsley plants may be allowed to stand 2 inches asunder. When they begin to crowd at this distance each second plant may be removed and sold. Four to six little plants make a bunch. The roots are left on. This thinning will not only aid the remaining plants, but should bring enough revenue to pay the cost, perhaps even a little more. The first cutting of leaves from plants of field-sown seed should be ready by midsummer, but as noted below it is usually best to practice the method that will hasten maturity and thus catch the best price. A "bunch" is about the amount that can be grasped between the thumb and the first finger, 10 to 15 stalks.

It is usual to divide the field into three parts so as to have a succession of cuttings. About three weeks are required for a new crop of leaves to grow and mature after the plants have been cut. Larger yields can be secured by cutting only the fully matured leaves, allowing the others to remain and develop for later cuttings. Three or four times as much can be gathered from a given area in this way. All plain leaves of such plants injure the appearance and reduce the price of the bunches when offered for sale.

If protected from frost, the plants will yield all winter. They may be easily transplanted in cold frames. These should be placed in some warm, sheltered spot and the plants set in them 4 by 6 inches. Mats or shutters will be needed in only the coldest weather. Half a dozen to a dozen stalks make the usual bunch and retail for 2 or 3 cents.

In the home garden, parsley may be sown as an edging for flower beds and borders. For such purpose it is best to sow the seed thickly during late October or November in double rows close together, say 3 or 4 inches. Sown at that time, the plants may be expected to appear earlier than if spring sown and to form a ribbon of verdure which will remain green not only all the growing season, but well into winter if desired. It is best, however, to dig them up in the fall and resow for the year succeeding.

For window culture, all that is needed is a box filled with rich soil. The roots may be dug in the fall and planted in the box. A sunny window is best, but any window will do. If space is at a premium, a nail keg may be made to yield a large amount of leaves. Not only may the tops be filled with plants, but the sides also. Holes should be bored in the staves about 4 inches apart. (See illustration, **page 2**.) A layer of earth is placed in the bottom as deep as the lowest tier of holes. Then roots are pushed through these holes and a second layer of earth put in. The process is repeated till the keg is full. Then plants are set on the top. As the keg is being filled the earth should be packed very firmly, both around the plants and in the keg. When full the soil should be thoroughly soaked and allowed to drain before being taken to the window. To insure a supply of water for all the plants, a short piece of pipe should be placed in the center of the keg so as to reach about half way toward the bottom. This will enable water to reach the plants placed in the lower tiers of holes. If the leaves look yellow at any time, they may need water or a little manure water.

As parsley is grown for its leaves, it can scarcely be over fertilized. Like cabbage, but, of course, upon a smaller scale, it is a gross feeder. It demands that plenty of nitrogenous food be in the soil. That is, the soil should be well supplied with humus, preferably derived from decaying leguminous crops or from stable manure. A favorite commercial fertilizer for parsley consists of 3 per cent nitrogen, 8 per cent potash and 9 per cent phosphoric acid applied in the drills at the rate of 600 to 900 pounds to the acre in two or three applications—especially the nitrogen, to supply which nitrate of soda is the most popular material.

A common practice among market gardeners in the neighborhood of New York has been to sow the seed in their cold frames between rows of lettuce transplanted during March or early April. The lettuce is cut in May, by which time the parsley is getting up. When grown by this plan the crop may be secured four or five weeks earlier than if the seed is sown in the open ground. The first cutting may be made during June. After this first cutting has been made the market usually becomes overstocked and the price falls, so many growers do not cut again until early September when they cut and destroy the leaves preparatory to securing an autumn and winter supply.

When the weather becomes cool and when the plants have developed a new and sturdy rosette of leaves, they are transplanted in shallow trenches either in cold frames, in cool greenhouses (lettuce and violet houses), under the benches of greenhouses, or, in fact, any convenient place that is not likely to prove satisfactory for growing plants that require more heat and light.

This method, it must be said, is not now as popular near the large cities as before the development of the great trucking fields in the Atlantic coast states; but it is a thoroughly practical plan and well worth practicing in the neighborhood of smaller cities and towns not adequately supplied with this garnishing and flavoring herb.

A fair return from a cold frame to which the plants have been transplanted ranges from $3 to $7 during the winter months. Since many sashes are stored during this season, such a possible return deserves to be considered. The total annual yield from an acre by this method may vary from $500 to $800 or even more—gross. By the ordinary field method from $150 to $300 is the usual range. Instead of throwing away the leaves cut in September, it should be profitable to dry these leaves and sell them in tins or jars for flavoring.

When it is desired to supply the demand for American seed, which is preferred to European, the plants may be managed in any of the ways already mentioned, either allowed to remain in the field or transplanted to cold frames, or greenhouses. If left in the field, they should be partially buried with litter or coarse manure. As the ground will not be occupied more than a third of the second season, a crop of early beets, forcing carrots, radishes, lettuce or some other quick-maturing crop may be sown between the rows of parsley plants. Such crops will mature by the time the parsley seed is harvested in late May or early June, and the ground can then be plowed and fitted for some late crop such as early maturing but late-sown sweet corn, celery, dwarf peas, late beets or string beans.

When seed is desired, every imperfect or undesirable plant should be rooted out and destroyed, so that none but the best can fertilize each other. In early spring the litter must be either removed from the plants and the ground between the rows given a cultivation to loosen the surface, or it may be raked between the rows and allowed to remain until after seed harvest. In this latter case, of course, no other crop can be grown.

Like celery seed, parsley seed ripens very irregularly, some umbels being ready to cut from one to three weeks earlier than others. This quality of the plant may be bred out by keeping the earliest maturing seed separate from the later maturing and choosing this for producing subsequent seed crops. By such selection one to three weeks may be saved in later seasons, a saving of time not to be ignored in gardening operations.

In ordinary seed production the heads are cut when the bulk of the seed is brown or at least dark colored. The stalks are cut carefully, to avoid shattering the seed off. They are laid upon sheets of duck or canvas and threshed very lightly, at once, to remove only the ripest seed. Then the stalks are spread thinly on shutters or sheets in the sun for two days and threshed again. At that time all seed ripe enough to germinate will fall off. Both lots of seed must be spread thinly on the sheets in an airy shed or loft and turned daily for 10 days or two weeks to make sure they are thoroughly dry before being screened in a fanning mill and stored in sacks hung in a loft.

Varieties.—There are four well-defined groups of parsley varieties; common or plain, curled or moss-leaved, fern-leaved, and Hamburg. The last is also known as turnip-rooted or large-rooted. The objections to plain parsley are that it is not as ornamental as moss-leaved or fern-leaved sorts, and because it may be mistaken for fools parsley, a plant reputed to be more or less poisonous.

In the curled varieties the leaves are more or less deeply cut and the segments reflexed to a greater or less extent, sometimes even to the extent of showing the lighter green undersides. In this group are several subvarieties, distinguished by minor differences, such as extent of reflexing and size of the plants.

In the fern-leaved group the very dark green leaves are not curled but divided into numerous threadlike segments which give the plant a very delicate and dainty appearance.

Hamburg, turnip-rooted or large-rooted parsley, is little grown in America. It is not used as a garnish or an herb, but the root is cooked as a vegetable like carrots or beets. These roots resemble those of parsnips. They are often 6 inches long and 2 inches in diameter. Their cultivation is like that of parsnips. They are cooked and served like carrots. In flavor, they resemble celeriac or turnip-rooted celery, but are not so pleasing. In Germany the plant is rather popular, but, except by our German gardeners, it has been little cultivated in this country.

Uses.—The Germans use both roots and tops for cooking; the former as a boiled vegetable, the latter as a potherb. In English cookery the leaves are more extensively used for seasoning fricassees and dressings for mild meats, such as chicken and veal, than perhaps anything else. In American cookery parsley is also popular for this purpose, but is most extensively used as a garnish. In many countries the green leaves are mixed with salads to add flavor. Often, especially among the Germans, the minced green leaves are mixed with other vegetables just before being served. For instance, if a liberal dusting of finely minced parsley be added to peeled, boiled potatoes, immediately after draining, this vegetable will seem like a new dish of unusual delicacy. The potatoes may be either served whole or mashed with a little butter, milk and pepper.

Pennyroyal (*Mentha Pulegium*, Linn.), a perennial herb of the natural order Labiatæ, native of Europe and parts of Asia, found wild and naturalized throughout the civilized world in strong, moist soil on the borders of ponds and streams. Its square, prostrate stems, which readily take root at the nodes, bear roundish-oval, grayish-green, slightly hairy leaves and small lilac-blue flowers in whorled clusters of ten or a dozen, rising in tiers, one above another, at the nodes. The seed is light brown, oval and very small. Like most of its near relatives, pennyroyal is highly aromatic, perhaps even more so than any other mint. The flavor is more pungent and acrid and less agreeable than that of spearmint or peppermint.

Ordinarily the plant is propagated by division like mint, or more rarely by cuttings. Cultivation is the same as that of mint. Plantations generally last for four or five years, and even longer, when well managed and on favorable soil. In England it is more extensively cultivated than in America for drying and for its oil, of which latter a yield of 12 pounds to the acre is considered good. The leaves, green or dried, are used abroad to flavor puddings and other culinary preparations, but the taste and odor are usually not pleasant to American and English palates and noses.

Peppermint (*Mentha piperita*, Linn.) is much the same in habit of growth as spearmint. It is a native of northern Europe, where it may be found in moist situations along stream banks and in waste lands. In America it is probably even more common as an escape than spearmint. Like its relative, it has long been known and grown in gardens and fields, especially in Europe, Asia and the United States.

Description.—Like spearmint, the plant has creeping rootstocks, which rapidly extend it, and often make it a troublesome weed in moist ground. The stems are smaller than those of spearmint, not so tall, and are more purplish. They bear ovate, smooth leaves upon longer stalks than those of spearmint. The whorled clusters of little, reddish-violet flowers form loose, interrupted spikes. No seed is borne.

Cultivation.—Although peppermint prefers wet, even swampy, soil, it will do well on moist loam. It is cultivated like spearmint. In Michigan, western New York and other parts of the country it is grown commercially upon muck lands for the oil distilled from its leaves and stems. Among essential oils, peppermint ranks first in importance. It is a colorless, yellowish or greenish liquid, with a peculiar, highly penetrating odor and a burning, camphorescent taste. An interesting use is made of it by sanitary engineers, who test the tightness of pipe joints by its aid. It has the faculty of making its escape and betraying the presence of leaks. It is largely employed in the manufacture of soaps and perfumery, but probably its best known use is for flavoring confectionery.

Rosemary (*Rosemarinus officinalis*, Linn.) — As its generic name implies, rosemary is a native of sea-coasts, "rose" coming from *Ros*, dew, and "Mary" from *marinus*, ocean. It is one of the many Labiatæ found wild in limy situations along the Mediterranean coast. In ancient times many and varied virtues were ascribed to the plant, hence its "officinalis" or medical name, perhaps also the belief that "where rosemary flourishes, the lady rules!" Pliny, Dioscorides and Galin all write about it. It was cultivated by the Spaniards in the 13th century, and from the 15th to the 18th century was popular as a condiment with salt meats, but has since declined in popularity, until now it is used for seasoning almost exclusively in Italian, French, Spanish and German cookery.

Description. — The plant is a half-hardy evergreen, 2 feet or more tall. The erect, branching, woody stems bear a profusion of little obtuse, linear leaves, green above and hoary white beneath. On their upper parts they bear pale blue, axillary flowers in leafy clusters. The light-brown seeds, white where they were attached to the plant, will germinate even when four years old. All parts of the plant are fragrant—"the humble rosemary whose sweets so thanklessly are shed to scent the desert" (Thomas Moore). One of the pleasing superstitions connected with this plant is that it strengthens the memory. Thus it has become the emblem of remembrance and fidelity. Hence the origin of the old custom of wearing it at weddings in many parts of Europe.

"There's rosemary, that's for remembrance; pray, love, remember:
And there is pansies, that's for thoughts."

—Hamlet, Act iv, Scene 5.

Cultivation.—Rosemary is easily propagated by means of cuttings, root division and layers in early spring, but is most frequently multiplied by seed. It does best in rather poor, light soil, especially if limy. The seed is either sown in drills 18 to 24 inches apart or in checks 2 feet asunder each way, half a dozen seeds being dropped in each "hill." Sometimes the seedbed method is employed, the seed being sown either under glass or in the open ground and the seedlings transplanted. Cultivation consists in keeping the soil loose and open and free from weeds. No special directions are necessary as to curing. In frostless sections, and even where protected by buildings, fences, etc., in moderate climates, the plants will continue to thrive for years.

Uses.—The tender leaves and stems and the flowers are used for flavoring stews, fish and meat sauces, but are not widely popular in America. Our foreign-born population, however, uses it somewhat. In France large quantities, both cultivated and wild, are used for distilling the oil of rosemary, a colorless or yellowish liquid suggesting camphor, but even more pleasant. This oil is extensively used in perfuming soaps, but more especially in the manufacture of eau de cologne, Hungary water and other perfumes.

Rue (*Ruta graveolens*, Linn.), a hardy perennial herb of roundish, bushy habit, native of southern Europe. It is a member of the same botanical family as the orange, Rutaceæ. In olden times it was highly reputed for seasoning and for medicine among the Greeks and the Romans. In Pliny's time it was considered to be effectual for 84 maladies! Today it "hangs only by its eyelids" to our pharmacopœia. Apicus notes it among the condiments in the third century, and Magnus eleven centuries later praises it among the garden esculents. At present it is little used for seasoning, even by the Italians and the Germans, and almost not at all by English and American cooks. Probably because of its acridity and its ability to blister the skin when much handled, rue has been chosen by poets to express disdain. Shakespeare speaks of it as the "sour herb of grace," and Theudobach says:

> "When a rose is too haughty for heaven's dew
> She becometh a spider's gray lair;
> And a bosom, that never devotion knew
> Or affection divine, shall be filled with rue
> And with darkness, and end with despair."

Description.—The much branched stems, woody below, rise 18 to 24 inches and bear small oblong or obovate, stalked, bluish-green glaucous leaves, two or three times divided, the terminal one broader and notched at the end. The rather large, greenish-yellow flowers, borne in corymbs or short terminal clusters, appear all summer. In the round, four or five-lobed seed vessels are black kidney-shaped seeds, which retain their vitality two years or even longer. The whole plant has a very acrid, bitter taste and a pungent smell.

Cultivation.—The plant may be readily propagated by means of seed, by cuttings, by layers, and by division of the tufts. No special directions are needed, except to say that when in the place they are to remain the plants should be at least 18 inches apart—21 or 24 inches each way would be even better. Rue does well on almost any well-drained soil, but prefers a rather poor clayey loam. It is well, then, to plant it in the most barren part of the garden. As the flowers are rather attractive, rue is often used among shrubbery for ornamental purposes. When so grown it is well to cut the stems close to the ground every two or three years.

Rue, Sour Herb of Grace

Uses.—Because of the exceedingly strong smell of the leaves, rue is disagreeable to most Americans, and could not become popular as a seasoning. Yet it is used to a small extent by people who like bitter flavors, not only in culinary preparations, but in beverages. The whole plant is used in distilling a colorless oil which is used in making aromatic vinegars and other toilet preparations. A pound of oil may be secured from 150 to 200 pounds of the plant.

Sage (*Salvia officinalis*, Linn.), a perennial member of the Labiatæ, found naturally on dry, calcareous hills in southern Europe, and northern Africa. In ancient times, it was one of the most highly esteemed of all plants because of its reputed health-insuring properties. An old adage reads, "How can a man die in whose garden sage is growing?" Its very names betoken the high regard in which it was held; salvia is derived from *salvus*, to be safe, or *salveo*, to be in good health or to heal; (hence also salvation!) and *officinalis* stamps its authority or indicates its recognized official standing. The name sage, meaning wisdom, appears to have had a different origin, but as the plant was reputed to strengthen the memory, there seems to be ground for believing that those who ate the plant would be wise.

Description.—The almost woody stems rise usually 15 to 18 inches high, though in Holt's Mammoth double these sizes is not uncommon. The leaves are oblong, pale green, finely toothed, lance-shaped, wrinkled and rough. The usually bluish-lilac, sometimes pink or white flowers, borne in the axils of the upper leaves in whorls of three or four, form loose terminal spikes or clusters. Over 7,000 of the small globular, almost black seeds, which retain their vitality about three years, are required to weigh an ounce, and nearly 20 ounces to the quart.

Cultivation.—Sage does best upon mellow well-drained soil of moderate fertility. For cultivation on a large scale the soil should be plowed deeply and allowed to remain in the rough furrows during the winter, to be broken up as much as possible by the frost. In the spring it should be fined for the crop. Sage is easily propagated by division, layers and cuttings, but these ways are practiced on an extensive scale only with the Holt's Mammoth variety, which produces no seed. For other varieties seed is most popular. This is sown in drills at the rate of two seeds to the inch and covered about ¼ inch deep. At this rate and in rows 15 inches apart about 8 pounds of seed will be needed to the acre.

Sage, the Leading Herb for Duck and Goose Dressing

Usually market gardeners prefer to grow sage as a second crop. They therefore raise the plants in nursery beds. The seed is sown in very early spring, not thicker than already mentioned, but in rows closer together, 6 to 9 inches usually. From the start the seedlings are kept clean cultivated and encouraged to grow stocky. By late May or early June the first sowings of summer vegetables will have been marketed and the ground ready for the sage. The ground is then put in good condition and the sage seedlings transplanted 6 or 8 inches apart usually. Clean cultivation is maintained until the sage has possession.

When the plants meet, usually during late August, the alternate ones are cut, bunched and sold. At this time one plant should make a good bunch. When the rows meet in mid-September, the alternate rows are marketed, a plant then making about two bunches. By the middle of October the final cutting may be started, when the remaining plants should be large enough to make about three bunches each. This last cutting may continue well into November without serious loss of lower leaves. If the plants are not thinned, but are allowed to crowd, the lower leaves will turn yellow and drop off, thus entailing loss.

**Relative Sizes of
Holt's Mammoth and Common
Sage Leaves**

For cultivation with hand-wheel hoes the plants in the rows should not stand closer than 2 inches at first. As soon as they touch, each second one should be removed and this process repeated till, when growing in a commercial way, each alternate row has been removed. Finally, the plants should be 12 to 15 inches apart. For cultivation by horse the rows will need to be farther apart than already noted; 18 to 24 inches is the usual range of distances. When grown on a large scale, sage usually follows field-grown lettuce, early peas or early cabbage. If not cut too closely or too late in the season sage plants stand a fair chance to survive moderate winters. The specimens which succeed in doing so may be divided and transplanted to new soil with little trouble. This is the common practice in home gardens, and is usually more satisfactory than growing a new lot of plants from seed each spring.

For drying or for decocting the leaves are cut when the flowers appear. They are dried in the shade. If a second cutting is to be made, and if it is desired that the plants shall live over winter, this second cutting must not be made later than September in the North, because the new stems will not have time to mature before frost, and the plants will probably winterkill.

Sage seed is produced in open cups on slender branches, which grow well above the leaves. It turns black when ripe. The stems which bear it should be cut during a dry afternoon as soon as the seeds are ripe and placed on sheets to cure; and several cuttings are necessary, because the seed ripens unevenly. When any one lot of stems on a sheet is dry a light flail or a rod will serve to beat the seed loose. Then small sieves and a gentle breeze will separate the seed from the trash. After screening the seed should be spread on a sheet in a warm, airy place for a week or so to dry still more before being stored in cloth sacks. A fair yield of leaves may be secured after seed has been gathered.

Uses.—Because of their highly aromatic odor sage leaves have long been used for seasoning dressings, especially to disguise the too great lusciousness of strong meats, such as pork, goose and duck. It is one of the most important flavoring ingredients in certain kinds of sausage and cheese. In France the whole herb is used to distill with water in order to secure essential oil of sage, a greenish-yellow liquid employed in perfumery. About 300 pounds of the stems and leaves yield one pound of oil.

Samphire (*Crithmum maritimum*, Linn.), a European perennial of the Umbelliferæ, common along rocky sea coasts and cliffs beyond the reach of the tide. From its creeping rootstocks short, sturdy, more or less widely branched stems arise. These bear two or three thick, fleshy segmented leaves and umbels of small whitish flowers, followed by yellow, elliptical, convex, ribbed, very light seeds, which rarely retain their germinating power more than a year. In gardens the seed is therefore generally sown in the autumn as soon as mature in fairly rich, light, well-drained loam. The seedlings should be protected with a mulch of straw, leaves or other material during winter. After the removal of the mulch in the spring no special care is needed in cultivation. The young, tender, aromatic and saline leaves and shoots are pickled in vinegar, either alone or with other vegetables.

Dainty Summer Savory

Savory, Summer (*Satureia hortensis*, Linn.), a little annual plant of the natural order Labiatæ indigenous to Mediterranean countries and known as an escape from gardens in various parts of the world. In America, it is occasionally found wild on dry, poor soils in Ohio, Illinois, and some of the western states. The generic name is derived from an old Arabic name, *Ssattar*, by which the whole mint family was known. Among the Romans both summer and winter savory were popular 2,000 years ago, not only for flavoring, but as potherbs. During the middle ages and until the 18th century it still maintained this popularity. Up to about 100 years ago it was used in cakes, puddings and confections, but these uses have declined.

Description.—The plant, which rarely exceeds 12 inches in height, has erect, branching, herbaceous stems, with oblong-linear leaves, tapering at their bases, and small pink or white flowers clustered in the axils of the upper leaves, forming penciled spikes. The small, brown, ovoid seeds retain their viability about three years. An ounce contains about 42,500 of them, and a quart 18 ounces.

Cultivation.—For earliest use the seed may be sown in a spent hotbed or a cold frame in late March, and the plants set in the open during May. Usually, however, it is sown in the garden or the field where the plants are to remain. In the hotbed the rows may be 3 or 4 inches apart; in the field they should be not less than 9 inches, and only this distance when hand wheel-hoes are to be used, and each alternate row is to be removed as soon as the plants begin to touch across the rows. Half a dozen seeds dropped to the inch is fairly thick sowing. As the seed is small, it must not be covered deeply; ¼ inch is ample. When the rows are 15 inches apart about 4 pounds of seed will be needed to the acre. For horse cultivation the drills should be 20 inches apart. Both summer and winter savory do well on rather poor dry soils. If started in hotbeds, the first plants may be gathered during May. Garden-sown seed will produce plants by June. For drying, the nearly mature stems should be cut just as the blossoms begin to appear. No special directions are needed as to drying. (See **page 22**.)

Uses.—Both summer and winter savory are used in flavoring salads, dressings, gravies, and sauces used with meats such as veal, pork, duck, and goose and for increasing the palatability of such preparations as croquettes, rissoles and stews. Summer savory is the better plant of the two and should be in every home garden.

Savory, Winter (*Satureia montana*, Linn.), a semi-hardy, perennial, very branching herb, native of southern Europe and northern Africa. Like summer savory, it has been used for flavoring for many centuries, but is not now as popular as formerly, nor is it as popular as summer savory.

Description.—The numerous woody, slender, spreading stems, often more than 15 inches tall, bear very acute, narrow, linear leaves and pale lilac, pink, or white flowers in axillary clusters. The brown, rather triangular seeds, which retain their vitality about three years, are smaller than those of summer savory. Over 70,000 are in an ounce, and it takes 15 ounces to fill a quart.

Cultivation.—Winter savory is readily propagated by means of cuttings, layers and division as well as seeds. No directions different from those relating to summer savory are necessary, except that seed of winter savory should be sown where the plants are to remain, because the seedlings do not stand transplanting very well. Seed is often sown in late summer where the climate is not severe or where winter protection is to be given. The plant is fairly hardy on dry soils. When once established it will live for several years.

To increase the yield the stems may be cut to within 4 or 5 inches of the ground when about ready to flower. New shoots will appear and may be cut in turn. For drying, the first cutting may be secured during July, the second in late August or September. In all respects winter savory is used like summer savory, but is considered inferior in flavor.

Southernwood (*Artemisia Abrotanum*, Linn.), a woody-stemmed perennial belonging to the Compositæ and a native of southern Europe. It grows from 2 to 4 feet tall, bears hairlike, highly aromatic leaves and heads of small yellow flowers. The plant is often found in old-fashioned gardens as an ornamental under the name of Old Man. In some countries the young shoots are used for flavoring cakes and other culinary preparations.

Tansy (*Tanacetum vulgare*, Linn.), a perennial of the Compositæ, native of Europe, whence it has spread with civilization as a weed almost all over the world. From the very persistent underground parts annual, usually unbranched stems, sometimes 3 feet tall, are produced in more or less abundance. They bear much-divided, oval, oblong leaves and numerous small, yellow flower-heads in usually crowded corymbs. The small, nearly conical seeds have five gray ribs and retain their germinability for about two years.

Tansy is easily propagated by division of the clumps or by seed sown in a hotbed for the transplanting of seedlings. It does well in any moderately fertile garden soil, but why anyone should grow it except for ornament, either in the garden or as an inedible garnish, is more than I can understand. While its odor is not exactly repulsive, its acrid, bitter taste is such that a nibble, certainly a single leaf, would last most people a lifetime. Yet some people use it to flavor puddings, omelettes, salads, stews and other culinary dishes. Surely a peculiar order of gustatory preference! It is said that donkeys will eat thistles, but I have never known them to eat tansy, and I am free to confess that I rather admire their preference for the thistles.

Tarragon, the French Chef's Delight

Tarragon (*Artemisia Dracunculus*, Linn.), a fairly hardy, herbaceous rather shrubby perennial of the Compositæ, supposed to be a native of southern Russia, Siberia, and Tartary, cultivated for scarcely more than 500 years for its leaves and tender shoots. In all civilized countries its popular name, like its specific name, means dragon, though why it should be so called is not clear.

Description.—The plant has numerous branching stems, which bear lance-shaped leaves and nowadays white, sterile flowers. Formerly the flowers were said to be fertile. No one should buy the seed offered as tarragon. It is probably that of a related plant which resembles tarragon in everything except flavor—which is absent! *Tagetes lucida*, which may be used as a substitute for true tarragon, is easily propagated by seed and can be procured from seedsmen under its own name. As tarragon flowers appear to be perfect, it is possible that some plants may produce a few seeds, and that plants raised from these seeds may repeat the wonder. Indeed, a variety which naturally produces seed may thus be developed and disseminated. Here is one of the possible opportunities for the herb grower to benefit his fellow-men.

Cultivation.—At present tarragon is propagated only by cuttings, layers and division. There is no difficulty in either process. The plant prefers dry, rather poor soil, in a warm situation. In cold climates it should be partially protected during the winter to prevent alternate freezing and thawing of both the soil and the plant. In moist and heavy soil it will winterkill. Strawy litter or conifer boughs will serve the purpose well. Half a dozen to a dozen plants will supply the needs of a family. As the plants spread a good deal and as they grow 15 to 18 inches tall, or even more, they should be set in rows 18 to 24 inches apart each way. In a short time they will take possession of the ground.

Uses.—The tender shoots and the young leaves are often used in salads, and with steaks, chops, etc., especially by the French. They are often used as an ingredient in pickles. Stews, soups, croquettes, and other meat preparations are also flavored with tarragon, and for flavoring fish sauces it is especially esteemed.

Probably the most popular way it is employed, however, is as a decoction in vinegar. For this purpose, the green parts are gathered preferably in the morning and after washing are placed in jars and covered with the best quality vinegar for a few days. The vinegar is then drawn off as needed. In France, the famous vinegar of Maille is made in this way.

The leaves may be dried in the usual way if desired. For this purpose they are gathered in midsummer. A second cutting may be made in late September or early October. Tarragon oil, which is used for perfuming toilet articles, is secured by distilling the green parts, from 300 to 500 pounds of which yield one pound of oil.

Thyme for Sausage

Thyme (*Thymus vulgaris*, Linn.), a very diminutive perennial shrub, of the natural order Labiatæ, native of dry, stony places on Mediterranean coasts, but found occasionally naturalized as an escape from gardens in civilized countries, both warm and cold. From early days it has been popularly grown for culinary purposes. The name is from the Greek word *thyo*, or sacrifice, because of its use as incense to perfume the temples. With the Romans it was very popular both in cookery and as a bee forage. Like its relatives sage and marjoram, it has practically disappeared from medicine, though formerly it was very popular because of its reputed properties.

Description.—The procumbent, branched, slender, woody stems, which seldom reach 12 inches, bear oblong, triangular, tapering leaves from ¼ to ½ inch long, green above and gray beneath. In the axils of the upper leaves are little pink or lilac flowers, which form whorls and loose, leafy spikes. The seeds, of which there are 170,000 to the ounce, and 24 ounces to the quart, retain their germinating power for three years.

Cultivation.—Thyme does best in a rather dry, moderately fertile, light soil well exposed to the sun. Cuttings, layers and divisions may be made, but the popular way to propagate is by seed. Because the seed is very small, it should be sown very shallow or only pressed upon the surface and then sprinkled with finely sifted soil. A small seedbed should be used in preference to sowing in the open ground first, because better attention can be given such little beds; second, because the area where the plants are ultimately to be can be used for an early-maturing crop. In the seedbed made out of doors in early spring, the drills may be made 4 to 6 inches apart and the seeds sown at the rate of 5 or 6 to the inch. A pound should produce enough plants for an acre. In hand sowing direct in the field, a fine dry sand is often thoroughly mixed with the seed to prevent too close planting. The proportion chosen is sometimes as great as four times as much sand as seed. Whether sown direct in the field or transplanted the plants should finally not stand closer than 8 inches—10 is preferred. When first set they may be half this distance. In a small way one plant to the square foot is a good rate to follow. The young plants may be set in the field during June, or even as late as July, preferably just before or just after a shower. The alternate plants may be removed in late August or early September, the alternate rows about three weeks later and the final crop in October.

Thyme will winter well. In home garden practice it may be treated like sage. In the coldest climates it may be mulched with leaves or litter to prevent undue thawing and freezing and consequent heaving of the soil. In the spring the plants should be dug, divided and reset in a new situation.

When seed is desired, the ripening tops must be cut frequently, because the plants mature very unevenly. But this method is often more wasteful than spreading cloths or sheets of paper beneath the plants and allowing the seed to drop in them as it ripens. Twice a day, preferably about noon, and in the late afternoon the plants should be gently jarred to make the ripe seeds fall into the sheets. What falls should then be collected and spread in a warm, airy room to dry thoroughly. When this method is practiced the stems are cut finally; that is, when the bulk of the seed has been gathered. They are dried, threshed or rubbed and the trash removed, by sifting. During damp weather the seed will not separate readily from the plants.

Of the common thyme there are two varieties: narrow-leaved and broad-leaved. The former, which has small grayish-green leaves, is more aromatic and pleasing than the latter, which, however, is much more popular, mainly because of its size, and not because of its superiority to the narrow-leaved kind. It is also known as winter or German thyme. The plant is taller and larger and has bigger leaves, flowers and seeds than the narrow-leaved variety and is decidedly more bitter.

Uses.—The green parts, either fresh, dried or in decoction, are used very extensively for flavoring soups, gravies, stews, sauces, forcemeats, sausages, dressings, etc. For drying, the tender stems are gathered after the dew is off and exposed to warm air in the shade. When crisp they are rubbed, the trash removed and the powder placed in stoppered bottles or tins. All parts of the plant are fragrant because of the volatile oil, which is commercially distilled mainly in France. About one per cent of the green parts is oil, which after distillation is at first a reddish-brown fluid. It loses its color on redistillation and becomes slightly less fragrant. Both grades of oil are used commercially in perfumery. In the oil are also crystals (thymol), which resemble camphor and because of their pleasant odor are used as a disinfectant where the strong-smelling carbolic acid would be objectionable.

Besides common thyme two other related species are cultivated to some extent for culinary purposes. Lemon thyme (*T. citriodorus*, Pers.), like its common relative, is a little undershrub, with procumbent stems and with a particularly pleasing fragrance. Wild thyme, or mother-of-thyme (*T. serpyllum*, Linn.), is a less grown perennial, with violet or pink flowers. It is occasionally seen in country home gardens, and is also used somewhat for seasoning.

www.ingramcontent.com/pod-product-compliance
Lightning Source LLC
Chambersburg PA
CBHW011256040426
42453CB00015B/2423